PLACE IN RETURN BOX to remove this checkout from your record.
TO AVOID FINES return on or before date due.

DATE DUE	DATE DUE	DATE DUE
JUN 2 1996		
NOV 0 2 1994		

MSU Is An Affirmative Action/Equal Opportunity Institution

c:\circ\datedue.pm3-p.1

THE POLITICS OF

PUNISHMENT

by

JOHN HOSTETTLER

JP, BA, LL.B. (Hons.), LL.M, Ph.D. (LOND)
A Solicitor of the Supreme Court

Publishers
Barry Rose Law Publishers Ltd
Chichester, England

Printed by Hobbs the Printers of Southampton

ISBN 1 87232812 1

Also by the author:

The Politics of Criminal Law: Reform in the Nineteenth
Century, 1992.

Thomas Wakley: An Improbable Radical, 1993.

Published by
Barry Rose Law Publishers Ltd
Chichester, England

CONTENTS

ABBREVIATIONS

Blackstone	Sir William Blackstone *Commentaries on the Laws of England,* vol.4.
BM Add. Mss.	British Museum Additional Manuscripts
Coke	Sir Edward Coke *3rd Institute* (1644)
Hale	Sir Matthew Hale *History of the Pleas of the Crown* (1736)
HO	Home Office Records
LQR	*Law Quarterly Review*
MLR	*Modern Law Review*
PP	Parliamentary Papers
PRO	Public Record Office
Stephen	Sir James Fitzjames Stephen *A History of the Criminal Law of England* (1883)

PREFACE

From the local public house to the Old Bailey everyone has an opinion about criminal law and punishments. Like the Common Law and Parliament many of our punishments have roots in the distant past. As a consequence the history of punishment is not only fascinating in itself but can cast a light on our present problems, not least because politics are an essential element in its fabric.

Until the Civil War in the seventeenth century, kings and their servants, the Judges, determined what acts would be crimes and what the punishments for them would be - usually bloodthirsty ones. Afterwards, and particularly following the Glorious Revolution in 1688, the aristocracy and the landed gentry captured that role and played a crucial part through Parliament and as Justices of the Peace. Then along with the dynamic changes wrought by the Industrial Revolution the rising middle class gave vent to a stirring nineteenth century movement for reform of the penal law along humanitarian lines.

As will be seen all were politically motivated, since the criminal law and punishments were considered to be instruments of power, legitimacy and social control. This was as true of the outstanding advocates of reform in the nineteenth century as of those concerned with ruling in the earlier periods going right back to Anglo-Saxon times.

Count Beccaria, Jeremy Bentham, William Eden, Sir Samuel Romilly, Sir Robert Peel and Lord Brougham were all part of the political scene. They had morality and public opinion on their side and they were passionately angry about the cruel punishments of the day. But their political motivation as part of a new force in a modern society was never obscured. As the Anglo-Saxon kings and Judge Jeffreys had earlier revealed, punishments and politics are interwoven and inseparable.

The scope of an investigation into the history of punishments through the ages is vast. In a book of this kind it is impossible to be all-embracing. However, I have preferred an outline of the whole to a more in-depth study of a particular period in an endeavour to capture the essential continuity of the process. Such a large canvass may mean that I have omitted certain cases or examples but I trust the book contains enough substance to excite the imagination.

Similarly, in the last chapter, on the ethics of punishment, I have not been able to deal with the full range of the literature on the subject but have attempted to unravel the secret hidden in the question ... Why punish?

It is a subtle and complex question and I have approached it, as far as anyone is able to, without too many pre-conceptions. I can only hope that the reader will share my enthusiasm for the project.

John Hostettler

'Cities and individuals alike, all are by nature disposed to do wrong and there is no law that will prevent it, as is shown by the fact that men have tried every kind of punishment ... in the attempt to find greater security from criminals ... It is impossible for human nature, when once seriously set upon a certain course, to be prevented from following that course by force of law or by any other means of intimidation whatever.'

Thucydides: *History of the Peloponnesian War.*
Penguin Classics. 220-21. 1972 edn.

'Law in a free country is, or ought to be, the Determination of the Majority of those who have Property in land.'

Jonathan Swift: *Thoughts on Various Subjects.*
245. 1957.

'As one reads history ... one is absolutely sickened, not by the crimes that the wicked have committed, but by the punishments that the good have inflicted.'

Oscar Wilde: *Soul of Man under Socialism.* Works. 922. 1963.

CHAPTER 1

ANGLO-SAXON ENGLAND

Pagan to Christian

Transgression and punishments have existed at all times and in all places. England is no exception but in the seventh century, when our law first began to emerge, legal restraint can only be described as primitive and harsh, as indeed was life itself. The times were wild. Men lived in terror of being robbed or slain, and of suffering famine or other disasters. Violence, death and superstition were rife. Murder and cattle-rustling were the most common outrages and they were dealt with in turn by private vengeance and constant blood-feuds, which led virtually to open warfare. Initially self-help was the only known law.

As time passed, kings and the Church took root and tried to enforce central political control over lawlessness. But the only answer they could find was to provide for cruel punishments and the merciless trial by ordeal. Rational means of determining guilt or innocence following an accusation were unknown.

When the Roman imperial occupation of Britain came to an end in 409 AD as the corrupt empire began to crumble, its renowned institutions, including villas, baths, religion and laws, evaporated with it. Its legacy of three centuries of civilization dissolved and what replaced it is largely shrouded in the impenetrable mists of the past. Evidence of history is found again only with the invasions of the Angles, Saxons and Jutes from northern Europe. These were heathen tribes and with good reason many of their warriors were called 'men of the long knives' by the native Britons. One group of them, the Engel, gave their name to the conquered country and by the year 603 Britain was no more.

The Jutes now ruled Kent, the Saxons controlled Wessex and the Angles governed Mercia and Northumbria to the north. There were originally seven Anglo-Saxon kingdoms but by the end of the sixth century these had merged into four confederations which, although exhibiting substantial differences in set-up, were significant powers with their own Teutonic religious customs and indistinct ideas of law. And although they started out as warring invaders they gradually began to settle into their new homelands as arable farmers.

Unlike the earlier Roman forms of society the new communities could boast little literacy, few officials and no central administration. But with exploitation of the agricultural fertility of the country, gradations of wealth and an aristocracy of the land began to emerge and each village community commenced to enforce, so far as it was able, its own peace and customs. No law or lawyers as we know them today existed but a system of self-protection evolved based on the vengeance of kin and neighbours against wrongdoers, usually accused of homicide or forcible breach of land tenures and boundaries.

At first few could write or keep records and there were no public officers to pursue or inquire into crime. Injuries inflicted were punished by private vendetta on the part of those who suffered from them and the vengeance was savage. Gradually, however, the rulers of the four kingdoms, whose powers were increasing and who could exercise direct personal control over their small populations, began to intervene against lawlessness and compose laws, known as dooms, written in English. Our knowledge of them remains fragmentary but they were created from existing customs and, after the reception of Christianity, were often directed not only against crime but also to securing obedience to the Church and augmenting its wealth. In return the Church underpinned the rule of the king and invested him with a religious aura.

Christianity managed to expand rapidly after 597, the year in which Augustine arrived in Kent to fulfil the mission of conversion entrusted to him by Pope Gregory the Great. Ethelbert, the king of Kent and southern England at that time, was already familiar with religious practices since his wife, Bertha, a princess from Paris, was a Christian and had been permitted to hold services in a church at Canterbury. Perhaps not surprisingly, therefore, Ethelbert's conversion was completed within a year and Augustine was rewarded with the church where he was consecrated a bishop and later appointed archbishop.

At Canterbury Augustine was able to rely upon royal support and protection which were not available in London, then part of Wessex and still heathen. Here too his 40 monks were given land and a dwelling place just outside the town from whence they could travel to preach their religion and disseminate the code of ecclesiastical law which Gregory had thoughtfully sent over with instructions to Augustine to keep his teachings flexible and take into account local customs.

Later, Paulinus, who had been consecrated bishop at Canterbury in 625, succeeded in converting Edwin the powerful king of Northumbria who had married Ethelburga, a daughter of Ethelbert, who fortunately was another Christian wife. Providentially Edwin also escaped from a treacherous attempt to murder him and enjoyed the support of a Witan sympathetic to the new religion. Wessex was finally brought into the fold under King Cynegils in 635, although there was to be some backsliding among succeeding kings and pagan rites would continue to persist throughout the country for some time to come.

Vengeance to Compensation

In the period after Ethelbert had embraced Christianity in Kent he enacted laws which are the earliest document we have written in English. By 689 Ine, who reigned as king of Wessex for 37 years, was also issuing an elaborate digest of West Saxon laws which comprised both ancient customs and new rules of conduct and punishments. Private vengeance by blood-feud was still countenanced, indeed it could hardly be stopped. But it was beginning to be seen as an interference with public peace and, in what was a breakthrough from the past, Ine endeavoured to curtail it.

Feuding parties were told to cease seeking blood and agree instead to a price to be paid in compensation for an injury. To cover cases where the parties could not agree on an amount in restitution the king set a tariff fixed according to the social status of the injured party. This was called *wergild* - a man's value. Nothing to do with the offender was taken into account. Intent was not inquired into, so an accidental injury was not excused, nor could any other extenuating circumstances be pleaded. They were just not conceived to be relevant.

The punishment was simply a penalty for an evil done and to deter from lawbreaking in the future. It took the form first of a civil indemnity, a *bot* - usually the wergild -

then, in many cases, a further indemnity, a *wite* - to the king. This payment to the king was another innovation and, with later additions, was to feed the wealth, and the growth, of royal power for centuries to come. It saw the beginning of the encroachment of political considerations into the arena of criminal justice with the Crown exerting more and more control.

As wergild was to persist for several centuries it may be useful to consider some features of social status in later Anglo-Saxon times. A noble by birth was called an *eorl*. Such a nobleman, and particularly the king, would have powerful household officers known as *thegns* who formed the landed gentry. Below them in rank were the *ceorls*, free peasant landholders who cultivated their holdings in person. In fact, a man was free precisely because of his ownership of land and in Ethelbert's time he was not subject to any lord but the king. Local lords of some power only began to appear on the scene when the kings started rewarding members of their households with grants of estates in land and large numbers of ceorls were reduced by hardship to villeinage.

Taxes for war and church dues could be crippling in hard times and, in particular, the ravages of the Viking invasions proved a disaster to an agricultural society. In consequence, an element of a peasantry of free men gradually lost its independence and under economic pressure became subject to lords and bound to weekly labour on their estates. In return they obtained some security but it was a hard price to pay.

Such villeinage was close to slavery but there was also a large unfree class of actual slaves. Initially they had been Britons but their numbers were augmented by criminals guilty of lesser crimes who were not put to death and prisoners from the endemic warfare of the times. Anathema though it may be today, slavery was fully recognized in Anglo-Saxon England with slaves being bought and sold openly, even by peasant farmers, and with a slave trade busy through the English ports. Indeed, selling a man abroad is found in the laws of Kent as an alternative to capital punishment, although later it became illegal to sell a Christian into slavery.

It should also be noticed on the point of status that the higher clergy not only had privileges which we shall examine later but they played an important role in government. They were close advisers to the king and exercised considerable influence in the framing of laws which they helped to enforce as leading members of the shire courts. At this stage there was no separation between ecclesiastical and secular jurisdictions.

The King's Peace

It is likely that in small communities the blood-feuds were sometimes influential as a means of preventing crime in that they would be known to produce instant reprisals. Equally, however, they could become self-feeding and lead to warfare and anarchy. The king's proclaimed scales of fixed compensation to avoid this were often doomed to failure as succeeding kings so often lamented when promulgating new sets of laws. And again status was important since, as with the tariff, men were not all equal in the blood-feud. For example, if one thegn was killed by a ceorl, his kin would demand the death of six ceorls. It will readily be perceived that such extensive blood-letting was a dangerous threat to the maintenance of law and order on which royal power rested.

At first compensation was believed to be the only possible alternative punishment to private vengeance. Hence Ine was not the only king to attempt to suppress this menacing feuding with a tariff. Alfred also tried, even in the midst of ferocious fighting to preserve his kingdom from the Danes. Edmund II went further and gave a killer 12 months in which to pay his wergild with a proviso that if he failed to pay within this extended time the feud was still not to proceed against his kindred, unless they had harboured him, on pain of outlawry.

Nevertheless, enforcing the king's law proved very difficult and, moreover, some crimes were coming to be seen as so serious that the state should intervene to punish those who committed them. This led to the gradual emergence of the concept of breaking the king's peace when for serious offences the wrongdoer was deemed to be *botless*. This meant that he could not redeem himself with compensation at all but was entirely at the mercy of the king. Such offences included treason to the king or one's lord, homicide and theft. The penalty was death.

Anglo-Saxon punishments henceforth were both plentiful and barbaric. They included death by hanging, beheading, burning and drowning; branding; the loss of hands, feet and tongue; eyes being plucked out; nose, ears and upper lip cut off; the scalp torn away; the body flayed alive; castration; and sale into slavery. In other words frightful torments inflicted by the state.

And, yet again, we witness the social class distinction. A nobleman could commit murder and still redeem himself with one fine to the Church and another to be divided between the kin of the slain and the king. For a slave, a free man of low estate and a woman, on the other hand, the penalty was one of the awesome deaths mentioned above. For minor offences, such as being a scold, a ducking stool fixed over a pond would be used and the pillory and stocks were also known. These too were sometimes known to result in death.

Communal Courts

Perhaps at this point something should be said of the Anglo-Saxon courts and how they arbitrarily determined guilt or innocence. Always bearing in mind, as with crimes and punishments, that society and law were not static but were evolving, albeit slowly, throughout this 500-year period. From early times England was divided into shires, most of which are still with us, and each shire was divided into hundreds.

These hundreds were districts probably equivalent to one hundred hides, each of which was the landholding of a normal peasant. In much of the country such a hide covered roughly 120 arable acres although the acreage could vary and was only 40 in Wessex. Within each hundred there would be a number of villages which would comprise a group of wooden homesteads with sheds for cattle, and barns. There would be few roads. Even a palace of the king was no more than a long wooden hall with a large number of outhouses.

The shires held county courts under the presidency of an eorl and a bishop until the reign of William the Conqueror when the Church was given its own courts to deal with ecclesiastical issues. Shire courts were held in public and at first met twice a year for one day, but as the law expanded they met monthly. Proceedings were oral, no records were kept, and initially they sat out of doors until later moving into a castle or shire hall. Their remit was to deal with cases of murder, theft, affray and wounding.

There were also hundred courts (known as wapentakes in areas of the country conquered by the Danes) which met every four weeks, again in the open air. These were local popular assemblies, quasi-democratic in nature. They adjusted taxation with the officials of the king, maintained peace and order when they could, and settled local disputes. The sheriff presided as the king's agent and collector of profits, but not as a Judge.

Nonetheless, important though they were, these courts were not generally held in awe by criminals and they had few means of compelling obedience. Very few lawbreakers were caught and as a consequence if a ceorl left his home without explanation he would be assumed to be guilty of an offence and could be summarily hanged. And Alfred had no hesitation in following the maxims of an eye for an eye and a tooth for a tooth in endeavouring to ensure compliance with his laws.

In what was a rough age, crime and violence were regarded as normal. As we have seen, the most common crimes were homicide, wounding and cattle-theft. So frequent was the last of these that many laws were enacted to ensure that the sale and purchase of cattle, and sometimes other chattels, did not take place without the presence of responsible witnesses. And if a man set out on a journey to make such a purchase he was also obliged to inform his neighbours in advance of his intent and on his return reveal his purchase to them if he had been successful.

When a thief was detected in the act of carrying away what he had stolen there would be no trial but an immediate fine or, if he was poor, death. If a thief or a murderer escaped, a "hue and cry" would be raised with much shouting and banging of utensils, and if he were sighted he could be killed on the spot. Were the "hue and cry" not to succeed in tracking down the offender he would be declared an outlaw, which automatically sanctioned his being killed at any time, with impunity and without repercussion, like a wild beast. In the meantime his kin would be fined. An alleged offender who refused to attend court on three occasions would also find himself declared an outlaw.

Oaths and Ordeals

Once an accused was before the court, which was composed of respected representatives of the people at large, there could be no trial on questions of fact - such a process was unknown. He was there on suspicion of criminal activity and had to seek a verdict from the Almighty by means of oath-helpers or endure trial by ordeal. If he could produce sufficient oath-helpers (known as compurgators) to vouch for his character that was deemed conclusive evidence from the Almighty of his innocence.

On the other hand, if he were unable to find enough oath-helpers, he had to undergo the ordeal which was also a judgment of God. Anglo-Saxon men sitting as a court did not even consider that they had the ability to determine questions of guilt and innocence without divine intervention and miraculous guidance.

For most people life was arduous in those times and trial by ordeal reflected that harshness. Like so much else in Christian countries it was of heathen origin but had been adapted to the use of the Church. It could take various forms but was always a religious ceremony. Indeed, King Ine's laws claimed that the rituals were laid down according to the commands of God, the archbishop and all the bishops.

One ritual was known as the ordeal by hot water. For this an iron cauldron was placed over a fire in a church. When the water boiled the accused had to reach down into the vessel and snatch up a stone from the bottom. If the accusation was of a minor offence the hand was plunged in only up to the wrist. If a serious crime was involved it went in up to the elbow. Presumably different sizes of cauldron were used in each case. The hand or arm was then swathed in cloth or linen for three days, after which it would be exposed and if the flesh was uninjured

God had pronounced the accused not guilty. If the flesh was scalded he was guilty and was sentenced by the court, usually to death.

In the ordeal by hot iron the suspect had to lift a piece of red-hot metal, weighing either one or three pounds according to the seriousness of the alleged offence, and carry it over a distance of nine paces. The hand would then be bound in a manner similar to that with the ordeal of hot water. If the hand of the accused healed within three days the verdict of God was - innocent. If it was festering the accused was guilty and punished accordingly. The church in which these dramas took place would be lined on each side with men who had come to see that the ordeal was performed fairly. Each was forbidden to eat food or sleep with his wife during the previous evening. And before the ordeal could take place he would have to kiss the Bible and make the sign of the cross.

Another ritual of trial by ordeal involved the suspect walking barefoot and blindfold over nine red-hot ploughshares. If he completed the walk unharmed the verdict was not guilty. Emma, the mother of Edward the Confessor, is said to have undergone this ordeal when he accused her of adultery with the Bishop of Winchester. She appears to have emerged from it successfully.

The ordeal of cold water, which was normally reserved for persons without rank, involved casting the bound body of the accused into a pond or river near the church, after he had been given holy water to drink. If he floated he was considered to be swimming away and hence guilty. If he sank he was innocent, which would not help him unless he was fished out in time.

For the clergy the ordeal meant swallowing an ounce of consecrated barley bread, or an ounce of cheese, impregnated with a feather. If the suspect choked that was held to be proof from God of guilt. Sometimes this

ordeal was prescribed for non-clerics. Godwin, the father
of King Harold, was subjected to it when accused of
murdering his brother. "May this bread choke me if I am
guilty" he cried, and promptly fell down dead.

What needs to be remembered is that all these ordeals
were inflicted not as punishments - no final verdict had
yet been reached - but as trials. And the clergy had entire
control over the conduct of them. This included, for
example, deciding on the quality of the bandage in the
ordeals of hot water and iron, the timing of the attempt
to rescue the innocent in the ordeal by cold water and the
size of the feather inside the bread or cheese. It is a
matter of conjecture whether they endeavoured to
mitigate the terrors of the various ordeals or turn them
into an almost certain death for enemies of the Church
or the priest, or perhaps both in different cases. It seems
unlikely that the witnesses brought in to ensure a fair
ordeal would have had much influence beyond confirming
that the weight of the iron or the bread was correct, if
even that.

Monarchy and Church

Once Christianity had become the dominant religion in
England by the year 663 there was no serious conflict
between secular and ecclesiastical authority. As we have
seen bishops and eorls presided over the shire courts and
the former had a large say in secular justice and
lawmaking. Furthermore, ecclesiastical pleas were heard
in the hundred courts. However, the king ultimately
controlled the Church by appointments to its higher
offices. And his laws secured substantial income not only
for the Crown but also for the Church by means of
plough-alms, tithes, and church-scot, which was a
payment in kind, often grain or livestock, levied on

freemen in proportion to the size of their holdings. Payment of all these dues was compulsory and heavy financial penalties for non-payment were disabling. In return, the Church continued to confirm that royal power was conferred by God. Once again we see the Church and Crown working in harness to maintain their hold both over the people and over the continuing flow of their ample revenues.

Generally speaking the power of the kings increased throughout the Anglo-Saxon period, but they were not autocrats and they were not sufficiently powerful to be able to forgo the support of the Church. They formed an elective monarchy and took advice on all important issues from the Great Council of the Realm, the *Witenagemot* or "Assembly of the Wise," which was originally a semi-democratic assembly which every freeman had the right to attend. By the time of Alfred the Great, however, it was normally composed of eorls, bishops and the wealthy aristocracy who together chose the king's successors.

All the dooms and laws that have come down to us are the enactments of the king backed by the Witan, as their preambles so often confirm. They did not attempt to replace ancient customs. What they normally did was to restate parts of the customary law in order to reinforce it and add new ordinances to meet changing conditions. In their preambles they also enunciated broad legal principles and objectives in the often vain hope that they would become widely observed.

CHAPTER 2

SAXON DOOMS - OUR EARLY LAWS

Written Law

The first written laws that have come down to us are those of Ethelbert. They contain 90 decrees in all.[1] The Church already took pride of place with a provision that thefts of the property of God and the Church were to be compensated twelve-fold. No doubt this was necessary to protect the newly arrived missionaries from Rome but it set an example which lasted for a long time to come.

The extensive fixed tariff of compensations which formed the attempt to replace the blood-feud was also clearly set out. It was decreed that if a man slew a freeman he should pay the slain man's wergild and, in addition, a fine of 50 shillings to the king. If a freeman robbed another freeman, usually of cattle, he had to pay threefold compensation and the king took a fine or all his goods. Already, in this early stage, we see the king using the law to enhance his own wealth by a supplement to taxation.

The burden of the wergild was extremely harsh since that of a freeman was one hundred gold shillings, equal

---

1.   These, and those of succeeding kings to the reign of Alfred, are to be found in F. Attenborough, (1922) *Laws of the Earliest English Kings*.

in value to the hundred oxen he was deemed to be worth. Twenty shillings had to be paid "before the grave was closed" and the remaining 80 within 40 days. If the slayer absconded his relatives were liable for half the wergild.

It is not easy to compare these values with those of today but, as a guide, a shilling would buy a sheep and six shillings an ox. And, by the twelfth century, a silver penny was the daily wage for a manual worker, with 12 pennies being equal to one shilling. Harsh though the penalty of wergild was, however, it was usually payable for homicide, although not exclusively, and was undoubtedly superior as a punishment to widespread revenge killing.

A further decree provided that if a freeman lay with the wife of another freeman the husband was not to kill him. Instead, the adulterer had to pay the husband his wergild of 100 shillings and then procure a second wife with his own money and deliver her to the husband's house. What happened to the first wife was not mentioned but these decrees were often somewhat ambiguous and in this case it may have been dealing with a wife who went to live with another man. We are also not told if the husband had any say in the choice of his second wife. If not, the procedure would have been open to intriguing abuse. Equally unclear is the influence of the Church on such laws.

For bodily injuries the compensation varied according to their seriousness. For example, a damaged bone was valued at four shillings, an eye knocked out at 50 shillings, a broken nose at nine shillings and destruction of the generative organ at 300 shillings. For these and other specific injuries the value could not be altered. By way of comparison with these fixed rates of compensation it can be noted that according to a Home Office Report in 1992 the *average* award by magistrates for a broken nose was £187, despite a guideline suggestion of between

£550 and £850. Often, the report complains, awards of as
little as £50 have been seen by magistrates as sufficient
full compensation for personal injuries.

Ethelbert also provided that the same amounts of
compensation should be paid to unmarried women but
nothing was said about wives. And when a man bought
a maiden in order to marry her, the bargain (whose was
not stated) stood if there was no dishonesty. On marriage,
a man was required to give his wife a "morning-gift" of
money and land. When a man died his widow was entitled
to half his property, as she was also if she left him with
her children during his lifetime - rare early examples of
property rights for women which were lost after the
Norman Conquest. These then give a flavour of
Ethelbert's laws, which were rather extraordinary for the
time, and the political climate in which they were
enacted.

Powers of Crown and Church

Of Ethelbert's successors as kings of Kent, Hhothhere and
Eadric, who may have ruled together, issued dooms but
in the main these followed the lines of those of Ethelbert.
Withred, however, in about 695 gave more favours to the
Church, although in the light of recent research there is
no certainty that all the Anglo-Saxon kings were devout
in their professed Christianity. The important thing to
them was the necessity of sharing power to underpin the
stability of both the Crown and the Church.

By this time, in Kent at least, the power of the Church
was comparable to that of the king, who was very largely
dependent on the assistance of literate clerical officials
to ensure that taxation was regarded as fair and was
efficiently collected. Only by mutual help could the
ascendancy of both the temporal and ecclesiastical rulers
be maintained and the political legitimacy of their control

over the lives of the people be demonstrated.

Whatever Withred's faith he formally enacted that the Church should enjoy immunity from taxation, which must have dented the desired perception of fairness. No doubt the power of the Church left him with little alternative. He also pioneered Sunday Observance laws. If a servant, contrary to his lord's command, did servile work between sunset on Saturday and sunset on Sunday it was decreed that he must pay 80 sceattas to his lord.

Twenty sceattas (later 20 silver pennies) equalled one Kentish shilling. The shilling was a silver or gold coin, the value of which varied from kingdom to kingdom. Payments of all kinds were often made by the weight of silver or gold, and the pound, shilling and penny were originally weights which survived until recently. Indeed, the pound and the penny coins are still with us for the time being. Only towards the end of the Anglo-Saxon period, however, was a single currency achieved, although Offa's penny held its value until the reign of Henry III - some 500 years.

Withred also decreed that if a servant made a journey on horseback on a Sunday he had to pay six shillings to his lord or, if he did not have the means to pay, suffer the lash. If a freeman worked on a Sunday he forfeited 20 shillings, of which half went to the informer, who was also rewarded with the wage or profit from the freeman's labour.

A husband and wife who made an offering to the devil had to pay a fine of 40 shillings or lose all their goods. If a man gave meat to his household during a religious fast he forfeited 20 shillings, and if a slave ate of his own free will at such a time he paid six shillings or suffered the lash. Further, the word of a bishop, like that of the king, was made incontrovertible even though unsupported by the sacred oath. More evidence, no doubt, that the Witan contained a good many clerics.

Ine and Alfred the Great

Let us leave Kent now and consider some of the laws of Wessex promulgated by Kings Ine and Alfred. Ine reigned from 688 to 725 when he abdicated and undertook a pilgrimage to Rome where he remained until his death. He too had to cope with a Witan which resembled a synod of bishops. All children were to be baptized within 30 days of their birth, failing which the parents paid a fine of 30 shillings. If a slave worked on a Sunday by his lord's command he automatically became a free man and the lord not only lost a slave but also forfeited 30 shillings. By contrast a freeman who worked on a Sunday was reduced to slavery if he could not pay a fine of 60 shillings, unless he had been obliged to work by his lord.

Anyone failing to pay his church dues not only forfeited 60 shillings but also had to pay the dues twelve-fold. There can be no doubt that church dues often impoverished peasant households in difficult years and, as with economic distress and the ravages of war, led many freemen to seek the security of servile status under a lord. On the secular side, any person who killed a reputed thief was allowed to declare on oath that the suspect was guilty whilst the family and friends of the slain man were not permitted an oath. Other decrees, of which there were 76 in all, were similar to those of the kings of Kent.

The next set of laws in Wessex were those of Alfred the Great who ruled from 871 to 900. His reign was a turning point in English history. He stemmed the tide of Danish invasions and showed that the Vikings could not only be defeated but also baptized. He recaptured London from them, built a navy on new lines and saved Wessex. With unsurpassed energy the hero king also managed to encourage learning and literature and it is no exaggeration to say that he brought about a revival of

English civilization. And in achieving all this he prepared the ground for the concept of one united kingdom of England.

So far as law is concerned, Alfred enacted the first Code for a century and a half, during which time the unremitting waves of Danish invasions had virtually broken down the machinery of law. In all, he enacted some 77 decrees with numerous sub-clauses, and he succeeded in integrating the English and Danish legal systems with an agreed scale of wergilds. The preamble to Alfred's laws contained a translation of the Ten Commandments into English, numerous passages from the book of Exodus, as well as a brief account of apostolic history. Many of the laws of Ethelbert, Ine and Offa (Offa's laws have been otherwise lost to us) were openly approved and restated with new additions. His councillors, Alfred declared, had approved of all that he had chosen.

He proudly proclaimed to all the Wessex hundreds that there was not to be one law for the rich and another for the poor. As with Ine's laws, it was made unlawful to commence a blood-feud before an attempt had been made to obtain compensation. And every man was required to abide by his oath and pledge. If he failed to carry out his pledge he was sent to a prison in a royal manor for 40 days.

If a man killed another unintentionally by allowing a tree to fall on him whilst they were engaged on a common task the tree was to be given to the dead man's kin. The tree was regarded as a guilty thing. It was the slayer, known to the law as a deodand. This must have been a fairly frequent occurrence to have been included in the laws but, of course, at this time much of the land was covered with forests which farmers would wish to cut back in order to make more arable land available. No one has so far discovered the origin of the ancient concept of deodand which is lost in the mists of antiquity.

Generally speaking a moving object such as a wheel, a horse or a cart which caused death was forfeit to the king even if the true cause of death was the negligence of an owner who had taken too much drink. The custom was that the king's almoner would distribute the value of the deodand for charitable purposes including compensating the family of the victim. But it was not seen primarily as a form of restitution, for which it was clearly inadequate, but according to Pollock and Maitland, "as an object upon which vengeance must be wreaked before the dead man will lie in peace."[2] Deodands survived until 1846 and we shall consider more of their curious history in later chapters.

Permitting a fugitive from justice to seek sanctuary in a church was another ancient custom incorporated into Alfred's laws. He also provided for compensation of six shillings for the first bite of a dog, 12 shillings for a second bite and 30 shillings for a third. Clearly the modern theory of allowing a dog a first bite without penalty does not have the blessing of Alfred, although some writers have fathered the concept on him.

In Wessex at this time a pound was made up of 48 shillings of five pennies each. The pound of 20 shillings of 12 pennies each, which survived until recently, was not to come until William the Conqueror. The penalty for public slander was the loss of the tongue. There was to be no vendetta or blood-feud against a man fighting another if he had found him with his wife, mother or daughter in bed or within closed doors, another example, by making a specific case, of how the general laws against feuding had not proved entirely successful.

---

2.   *The History of English Law.* ii. 474. 1968 edn.

Public Law

As a consequence of Alfred's military prowess and political wisdom the supremacy of Wessex over much of England was assured by the year 930. About this time King Athelstan enacted six new series of laws but, again, they did not replace earlier laws and customs. Athelstan did add, however, that no thief caught in the act was to be spared if he were over 12 years of age and the value of the stolen property was more than eight pence. Further, witchcraft, sorcery and deadly spells from which death resulted were made capital crimes. And a mere allegation might well be fatal when the only mode of trial for those with no compurgators to swear for them was the barbarous ordeal.

Innovative also was a law which established the *tithing*, whereby in every hundred, men were grouped into units of 10 with each such unit being held responsible for acts of wrongdoing by any one member of it. If the nine failed to take appropriate action they were to pay compensation personally for any damage the offender had caused, together with any fine imposed upon him. Unless exempted by wealth and high rank every man had to enrol in a tithing. Later this institution was to be widely used by William the Conqueror when a Norman was killed by someone unknown but presumed to be English.

Religious laws and ferocious punishments continued to loom large in the ordinances of subsequent kings. Edmund, who reigned from 939 to 946, enacted laws[3] in the preamble to which he declared that their purpose was to promote Christianity and bring to an end the manifold illegal deeds of violence which so distressed him. Tithes,

---

3.   For these laws and those of Edgar, Ethelred and Cnut *cf.* A.J. Robertson: *The Laws of the Kings of England from Edmund to Henry 1*. 1925.

church dues, Peter's Pence and plough-alms were to continue to be compulsory payments to the Church. The number of cases in which property was forfeit to the king was increased and was to include breaches of the king's peace, attacks on dwellinghouses and harbouring the kinsmen of those who had killed others.

Where a number of slaves committed theft the leader was to be slain without delay and each of the others scoured three times, have his scalp removed, and his little finger mutilated as a token of his guilt. King Edgar reinforced custom by an ordinance which provided that men belonging to the hundred should assemble every four weeks without fail. Heavy fines were to be paid for failing to respond immediately to a "hue and cry", and as theft was often of livestock articles of assistance in pursuit of a thief such as a cow's bell, a dog's collar and a horn were given a value of one shilling by law.

Another ordinance issued by Edgar, which he conceded was an attempt to enhance royal legitimacy, proclaimed that every man, rich or poor, was to enjoy the benefit of public law and be awarded just decisions. To that end if a Judge gave a false judgment he was to pay 120 shillings to the king as a penalty. As with all Anglo-Saxon laws we have little information as to how successfully this could be enforced and whether it caused the king to experience difficulty in finding sufficient Judges for the fairly new borough courts. The shire and hundred courts had no Judges as we have seen. In any event a false accusation before any court would result in the loss of the tongue or other severe punishment.

In another new departure from this time on, any party to a case could apply directly to the king if he failed to secure justice in his own locality. It is doubtful if this form of appeal could be easily exploited, although it should be borne in mind that throughout Anglo-Saxon times the king always possessed unlimited power of pardon. And the religious influence surfaces again. At one time in Edgar's reign a plague was raging. This, declared one of his decrees, was the consequence of sin. If tenants obstinately refused to pay their rents the lord was permitted to seize their property and their lives were forfeit. Likewise, tithes had to be paid to the Church or God would act in a similar manner.

Ethelred "The Unready"

Edgar died suddenly on July 8, 975. His eldest son, Edward the Martyr, was elected king by the Witan later in the same year but had ruled for less than three years when he was brutally assassinated by the retainers of his brother Ethelred at his step-mother's castle at Corfe in Dorset. He was succeeded by Ethelred who, as far as we know, was not directly implicated in the murder but who nevertheless bore the stigma of guilt that rocked the Crown and proved to be a weak king, known to history as "the Unready".

Ethelred's first laws were enacted at Wantage in Berkshire, then a royal manor and the birthplace of Alfred the Great. They constitute an important document in English legal history since they introduced the sworn jury to provide evidence, at that time with the majority prevailing. They also established that a breach of the peace could not be atoned for by compensation if the breach was confirmed by the king himself. This did not apply, however, in the Danish military centres known as the "Five Boroughs", namely, Derby, Leicester, Lincoln, Nottingham and Stamford, where 1,200 silver coins was the accepted fine for such a breach.

In London, by now an important trading town, Ethelred's laws provided that the gates at Aldersgate and Cripplegate were to be protected by guards and that ships calling at Billingsgate were to pay tolls.

Death with burial in an unconsecrated grave was to be the penalty countrywide for homicide, or assault on the king's highway. For trivial offences, on the other hand, Christians were not to be condemned to death but were to have "merciful" punishment which involved a payment of bot to the injured party and a wite to the king.

At all costs to be avoided, said the laws, were "untrue weights; false measures; horrible perjuries; devilish deeds such as murders, homicides, thefts and robberies; greed; gluttony and intemperance; frauds, breaches of law; violations of holy orders and of marriage; breaches of festivals and fasts; and misdeeds of many kinds." Wizards, sorcerers, magicians and prostitutes were to be driven from the land or executed, and the nation purified. From this extensive catalogue of crimes, misdemeanours and punishments it appears that at least Ethelred was not so unready when it came to extending the sweep of the criminal law as he may have been in resisting renewed Viking invasions.

Another side to these laws of Ethelred was the proclamation that so far as punishments were concerned not all persons were to be treated alike. This was a crucial advance on the earlier position that personal considerations, other than status, could not be taken into account when determining penalties. Perhaps the desire of the Church to save souls was having an influence on secular law. At all events the courts were now to bear in mind when fixing punishments the variables of age and youth, wealth and poverty, and health and sickness, as well as rank. In a startling breakthrough there was to be clemency for involuntary misdeeds and discrimination in judging every wrongdoing. Clearly new concepts of what law should be were filtering into the Anglo-Saxon mind.

Poacher Turned Gamekeeper

Finally, before the Norman Conquest ended 500 years of Anglo-Saxon rule, we should briefly consider the laws of Cnut, - "King of all England and the Danes" (1016-35). Cnut was the first king to compile a list of pleas of the crown - a concept which was to have far-reaching consequences in the future with the sovereign claiming to be injured by, and compensated for, every breach of public rights. These pleas included breach of the king's special peace, an attack on a dwellinghouse, ambush, concealing an outlaw and neglect of military duties.

Declaring that he had a special interest in such cases, Cnut had them brought directly before him or his sheriffs. He nourished a strong desire for extra sources of property and money, and forfeitures extended his estates whilst considerable numbers of fines went straight into his coffers. The result was that by now criminal justice and criminals had become an important source of Crown revenues - a process commenced by Ine but now expanded to a new level.

Cnut reiterated that all men, rich and poor alike, should enjoy the benefit of the law and that punishments were to be justifiable in the sight of God and acceptable in the eyes of men. They were to be merciful with no death for trivial offences. But apparently not too merciful since a woman who committed adultery was to lose her nose and her ears. Nothing was said of the man involved.

In the main, however, Cnut's Code (although usually so described, it was a code in name only and not in the technical sense of including all laws) was based on the earlier decrees of different kings and, as usual, included a great many customs. However, one important feature of Danelaw in the north of England was the provision that 12 senior thegns of each wapentake were from time to time to produce a list of notorious villains in their district. This bears a strong resemblance to the jury of presentment which came to prominence in the reign of Henry II and which had a similar task. It is considered by some legal historians to contain the seeds of our present trial by jury, although others maintain the jury had its origins in Germany. This dispute is unlikely ever to be resolved.

Cnut was king by violent conquest from Denmark. Nevertheless, he was anxious to establish his own legitimacy as the monarch of England with its flourishing agriculture, established towns and trade, and relatively advanced system of law. He was a classic example of poacher turned gamekeeper. This involved accepting and observing Anglo-Saxon laws and customs, and his Code remains the supreme relic of his reign from which it is clear that the ideal of the political unity of the whole of England had become familiar before the Conquest.

CHAPTER 3

NEW VENTURES IN THE CRIMINAL LAW

William the Conqueror

William I laid claim to England primarily by force of arms. He also pleaded direct descent from the Anglo-Saxon line of kings by way of gift from Edward the Confessor and election by the Witan. This was true in the letter but not in the spirit. When Edward, who by upbringing was more Norman than English, nominated William as his successor, the Witan had demurred, rightly claiming that kings were chosen by them and not designated by a predecessor. On Edward's death, just prior to which he had by now nominated Harold, the Witan formally elected Harold as king. However, after the Battle of Hastings they were left with little alternative but to confer the title on William who was anointed and crowned in Westminster Abbey on Christmas Day, 1066.

During his reign William took large estates of land from the English nobles and gave them to his Norman followers, to which the Domesday Book bears witness. On the other hand, he also provided England with strong central government. So far as law is concerned, Normandy had very little to offer, either customary or written, and English law was far superior to what there was. Hence, William had no incentive to change what he had inherited to any great extent and, in any event, he had nothing with which to replace it.

Like Cnut, he considered that adopting and keeping intact the existing law would confirm the legitimacy of his rule against his own rebellious noblemen, and he quickly issued a declaration that "we shall have and hold the law of King Edward." After all, he was king of England but only duke of Normandy. Among the few laws he framed himself Anglo-Saxon customs and the Code of Cnut loomed large. He confirmed the functions of the shire and hundred courts which continued to dispense justice in regard to crimes and punishments largely to the same extent as before. The foreign king also continued to retain many English royal advisers for a time, although by the end of his reign almost every lord and cleric was a Norman.

In only three areas of law did William make any substantial changes. First, he separated lay and ecclesiastical jurisdictions[1] by providing that the clergy should no longer hold spiritual pleas in the hundred courts or bring forward any such case for the judgment of laymen. From then onwards an accused cleric had to make amends before a bishop in accordance with canon law until, with royal sanction, Archbishop Lanfranc established church courts in 1077. Their jurisdiction was not confined to clerical misdeeds, however, but included matrimonial cases, adultery, usury, perjury and defamation - a jurisdiction they were to retain for centuries. This breach with Anglo-Saxon traditions was in accordance with Norman practice and it sowed the seeds of violent conflict to come between the Crown and the Church of a kind unknown in earlier times.

Secondly, the new king also introduced from Normandy

---

1.   Robertson. *The Law of the Kings of England.* 235.

trial by combat as an alternative to the ordeal.[2] This did not replace the ordeal but was seen as a further means of obtaining a judgment from God. An Englishman might summon a Norman to trial by battle and the Norman could not refuse. If the Englishman chose not to do so, however, the Norman could clear himself with an oath supported by his compurgators. On the other hand, if a Norman challenged an Englishman to trial by combat the Englishman had the choice of accepting and doing battle or undergoing the ordeal of iron.

For most criminal charges, including outlawry, the Normans chose trial by combat whilst Englishmen continued with the ordeal. Hence, in reality, combat was not imposed on the English, which was perhaps diplomatic on William's part. Nevertheless, as we have observed earlier, there was a special protection for the lives of Frenchmen since when one was killed by a person unknown a heavy fine, known as a *murdrum,* was imposed on the hundred where the murder took place on the legal presumption that the killer was English.

Thirdly, William abolished capital punishment. This was not out of humanitarian concern about the penalty of death, however, since he replaced it with blinding, castration, and other mutilations to the face and body in the belief that people who were thus maimed being seen at large would serve as a more lasting warning to would-be criminals than death. That this was the motive was confirmed when Lanfranc found it necessary to disassociate himself from such an idea at a synod in 1075. Nevertheless, the incidence of serious crimes had been reduced by the time of William's death, although other measures of such a powerful king may have contributed to that achievement.

William retained the Witan but converted it into a

---

2.   *Ibid.* 233.

royal council which he continued to consult on important
questions of state. However, he also established a royal
court with which he was more intimate and which, as the
Curia Regis, was destined to outlive the Witan and effect
vast changes in the English constitution. This was
composed of archbishops, bishops, abbots, earls, thegns
and knights, thus maintaining the political rule of the
secular authority and the Church in partnership. Shires
now became counties and earls as well as bishops ceased
to sit in the county courts where the sheriff became an
executive officer responsible only to the King.

The tithing gave rise to *frankpledge* which was a
compulsory fine fixed for individuals in each hundred
prior to any arrests but in anticipation of them. It was
probably introduced in order to protect Frenchmen living
in a hostile land. With some exceptions males over 12
years of age had to belong to the tithing and if an
offender, accused of any serious crime was not brought
to justice - which was frequently the case - the
frankpledge had to be paid by the members of his tithing
or village. In keeping with William's character this was
operated with more vigour than the Anglo-Saxon tithing
and to ensure that the system was working efficiently the
sheriff would preside over the hundred court twice a year
to "view the frankpledge."

Here, at what became known as the sheriff's tourn,
leading freemen from each village acted as presenting
juries as in the earlier wapentakes. Juries of 12 "hundred
men" considered any accusations made and if they
accepted them the suspects were arrested to face trial.
These presenting juries were the origin of the Grand Jury
which developed into a body of 24 men who, meeting in
secret, were to decide by a majority not if an accused was
guilty but whether there was sufficient evidence to justify
a trial. Later, as we shall see, it was from the Grand Jury
that members of the petty jury were selected to create the

form of trial that replaced the ordeal.

Following the death of the Conqueror in 1087 the succeeding reign of misrule by his son Rufus was one of cold comfort politically and was barren of new law. It was left to his younger son, Henry I, in his Coronation Charter, to reaffirm English law by restoring the laws of Edward the Confessor together with "the reforms introduced by my father." Despite this renewal, however, Edward's laws were in decline whilst, significantly, the king's council was taking on flesh and, at the same time, was in the process of becoming a court of law. Henry was the first king to send Judges through the counties to hear pleas of the Crown whilst the powerful in the land brought their disputes to him at Westminster.

The death penalty was restored and the king decreed that all thieves caught in the act should be hanged. Theft to the value of 12 pence or more also became a capital offence and remained so until 1827, despite the fall in the value of money during the intervening centuries. According to the *Anglo-Saxon Chronicle* on one day alone in the year 1124 Ralph Bassett, Henry's chief Judge, hanged 44 thieves in Leicestershire whilst six others lost their eyes and testicles.[3]

Anarchy

The Chronicle also tells us that in Stephen's reign of civil war and anarchy a new low was reached in the use of torture. According to an English monk named Laud, of the monastery of Peterborough, the barons, unrestrained by the king, enhanced their wealth by wanton savagery against the unhappy people of the country. Innocent men and women were flung into the prisons of the barons

---

3.   *Anglo-Saxon Chronicle.* 254.

where they were put to "unspeakable tortures" in order to lay hands on their gold and silver. He continues:

> They hung them up by the feet and smoked them with foul smoke. They strung them up by the thumbs, or by the head, and hung coats of mail on their feet. They tied knotted cords round their heads and twisted it till it entered the brain. They put them in dungeons wherein were adders and snakes and toads and so destroyed them. Some they put into a short, narrow, shallow chest into which they put sharp stones; and they crushed the man in it until they had broken every bone in his body ... They plundered and burned villages. It lasted throughout the 19 years that Stephen was king, and always grew worse and worse.[4]

It was fortunate for England that Stephen was succeeded by such a supreme legislator and administrator, so strong a king, as Henry II. Not that Henry consciously set out to change the face of English justice, but that is what he achieved with the form and content of both civil and criminal law. We are not here concerned with the momentous revolution he effected in the land law or its consequences but Henry made an equally significant impact on the administration of the criminal law. The truth is that the medieval political and economic conflicts were fought out on legal terrain and they are closely tied in with criminal justice.

Crown versus Church

In the first place the Crown and the Church came into serious conflict for the only time since the seventh century

---

4.   *Ibid.* 263.

as a consequence of the Conqueror embracing the idea of separate ecclesiastical courts. The trouble really commenced, when Henry was still a young man, with the Constitutions of Clarendon. During Stephen's "19 long winters" of anarchy not only the barons but the clergy also had seized the opportunity to increase their power in defiance of the law. Henry had no intention of ignoring the evasions of earlier laws, indeed he wanted to rely upon them in making a fresh start. First, however, he used Norman mercenaries to crush the lawless barons. He set about to restore the royal revenue, took back Crown lands from the barons, and destroyed many of their oppressive castles. Then he faced the task of grappling more peacefully with the encroachment on royal power by the Church.

After some bitter disputes with his former ally, Archbishop Thomas à Becket, Henry called together the Great Council of the Realm to meet at the royal palace of Clarendon in the New Forest in 1164. Here the king demanded that the bishops agree to respect the customs of the land, which recently they had formally declined to accept calling in aid their overriding duty to Rome or, as they put it, to God. Now they were required by the king to set their seals to a document containing 16 such customs - henceforth known as the Constitutions of Clarendon - which Henry claimed were only a restatement of the customs of his grandfather's time which the Church had always previously abided by.

At this stage, to everyone's surprise, Becket capitulated but only later to renege on his pledge and eventually to suffer martyrdom at the hands of four knights in Canterbury Cathedral. An essential element in the dispute was Becket's insistence that clerics should not have their crimes punished by the secular courts. This was a crucial issue on two counts. First, it is estimated that one in six of the population at that time was a cleric

if the lower orders are included, and criminal clerks guilty
of murder and rape proliferated. Secondly, if a cleric,
committed a serious crime it was only the secular courts
which could impose an appropriate punishment, the
penalties of the ecclesiastical courts being confined to
suspension from office or banishment from the altar.

Henry argued that once a cleric had been defrocked he
was no longer a clerk in holy orders and should be sent
to a secular court for a punishment to fit the crime. That
appears to be a sufficient reply to the suggestion of
Becket that clerics should not be punished twice for the
same offence, which Henry did not desire either. The
murder of Becket ensured his triumph on this issue with
the acceptance by Henry of the bizarre "Benefit of Clergy"
which was to bedevil the penal law for hundreds of years
to come. As late as the nineteenth century, Sir James
Fitzjames Stephen, an eminent authority on the criminal
law, was to claim that the benefit of clergy had for
centuries reduced the administration of justice to a
farce.[5]

At all events the "clergy" were now free from the
jurisdiction of the lay courts. Instead, a criminous clerk,
as he was called, would go before a bishop or his deputy
where he would state on oath that he was innocent. If 12
compurgators supported him he was acquitted. If not, he
was merely degraded or put to penance, even if he was
guilty of murder. Then, in 1350, in the reign of Edward
III, it was enacted that, "all manner of clerks, as well
secular as religious ... shall freely have and enjoy the
privileges of the Holy Church." This meant that assistants
to clerks such as doorkeepers, exorcists and sub-deacons
were henceforth to be treated as clergy.

For some reason the courts went even further and
extended the meaning of the Act to cover everyone who

---

5.   *History of the Criminal Law of England.* i. 463. 1883.

could read. The only test made of literacy, moreover, was an ability to read the first verse of the 51st psalm - appropriately known as the "neck-verse" - even if recited from memory by an illiterate person. The verse reads: "Have mercy on me, O God according to thy loving kindness; according to the multitude of thy tender mercies, blot out my transgressions." It was even known for Judges to send a prisoner who had been found guilty back to the cells to learn the verse before returning to the court to be set free.

It is apparent that this privilege would have startling consequences which will resurface later. Thinking of it as a merciful mitigation of harsh punishments, which to some extent it was, Blackstone wrote that the law "in the course of a long and laborious process, extracted by noble alchemy rich medicines out of poisonous ingredients."[6] Blackstone generally wore rose-tinted spectacles in regard to English law, however, and in reality numerous numbers of criminals escaped punishment and the "merciful mitigation" blunted any desire there might have been for reform of the penal law.

The King's Justice

To return to the laws of Henry II, we should bear in mind that crime was both brutal and rife and that Henry was determined to tackle it. Minor crimes could still be dealt with in the hundred courts and more serious crimes in the county courts. But Henry, the "lawyer king" was unifying English law into the common law by establishing a permanent body of professional Judges, by increasing the number of circuits of itinerant Judges and by introducing the germs of the new mode of trial by jury.

---

6. *Comm.* iv. 364.

As it was a form of royal justice the jury was never used in the communal courts which were beginning to wane. From this time onwards a crime was seen not merely as a wrong against the victim but against the nation.

Those accused of major crimes were most frequently brought to trial before the king's itinerant Judges. When these justices arrived in a district on their circuits, juries of presentment, made up of 12 neighbours elected from the hundreds and four from townships of the area, were put on oath to declare what crimes had been committed in their localities. They also had to indict before the Judges any persons suspected of serious crimes which the Assize of Clarendon (1166) pronounced to be murder, robbery, larceny, and harbouring criminals.

The punishments for these crimes were sanctioned by the state and anyone so indicted could be tried only by the Judges of the king who claimed for him all the forfeitures and fines which they imposed. To cope with the increased business the Assize also provided that public gaols and prisoners' cages had to be built in all districts for those awaiting trial. These were not meant for permanent imprisonment, however, since it was the duty of the Judges to empty the gaols by awarding other punishments, including death.

In the same year as the Assize Henry sent two senior Judges on a tour of the whole country to ensure that his wishes were carried out and to co-ordinate six trial circuits which were to have over 20 Judges. This led to the General Eyre which, over a period of years, visited each county in the realm to the dismay of law-abiding citizens. It dealt with all the outstanding criminal cases, which at the Eyre of Gloucester in 1221, for example, included 330 acts of homicide and 100 orders for outlawry.[7] The latter figure reveals the extent to which

---

7.   P & M. *Op. cit.*

criminals were able to evade capture for their crimes when policing was almost non-existent.

Apart from delivering the gaols, ie, trying those who had been arrested for committing crimes in the area, an Eyre also dealt with any misconduct brought to its notice including negligence by officials. So wide and deep were its inquiries, and consequent fines, that it reduced whole areas to poverty and at one time, in 1233, the men of Cornwall fled to the woods to avoid the forthcoming Eyre.

There was still no satisfactory means of finding the truth, however, and those who were accused were held in safe custody until being sent to the ordeal of cold water, where to be found innocent they had to run the risk of drowning. Even if, by the judgment of God, they were deemed innocent, they still had to leave the realm, so persuasive had the mere fact of an accusation become. If, on the other hand, they floated, and were thereby judged to be guilty, they were either hanged or lost a foot and were banished. A person was adjudged guilty in the ordeal if he floated in the belief that consecrated water would not receive a wicked body. Priests, it may be noted, were paid five shillings for preparing the pool and 20 shillings for blessing it.

In 1176, by the Assize of Northampton, treason, forgery and arson were added to the list of indictable crimes and the punishment was made even more severe with the loss of the right hand as well as a foot and banishment, if the criminal was not hanged. This Assize also put the *Curia Regis*, the King's Court, and the itinerant Judges' circuits on a permanent basis.

Once the ordeal was forbidden by the *Lateran* Council in 1215, and formally abolished in England in 1219 when Henry III was a boy king, it was only a short step for the Judges to ask the indicting, or presenting, jury if they thought the accused was guilty. Thus was trial by jury born instead of the inquisition of Continental countries, with Judges dependent on the jury in regard both to offences and offenders. In a sense there was a continuation of community involvement in which, at local and county level, lay judging was an integral part of royal justice.

Henry II, of course, was attempting to enforce a system of law and order but, like the Anglo-Saxon kings, he also saw the profitability of criminal justice in delivering revenue to the Crown. Hence, justice had to be paid for both by those seeking it and by those breaking its rules, and Henry's responses increased at an accelerating rate. Throughout his reign forfeitures and fines paid to the king were fast replacing the old tariffs of compensation. The king's Judges were now an established sight not only on their circuits but also at Westminster where the central court was busy consolidating a law common to the whole country. The criminal jurisdiction of the Crown had taken root nationwide.

At this time there was no legal distinction between murder and manslaughter. All homicides were murder except killings in self-defence or by accident, and even they needed a pardon from the king if the accused was to be set free. But it was a step in the right direction when, by c.9 of the Statute of Gloucester (1278) juries were required to state whether a homicide was murder or a killing by misadventure. As for punishment, a rapist would suffer castration and blinding, and after the Statute of Westminster of 1285, death. The penalty for arson was death by burning, as it was for a woman found guilty of any serious crime.

Hanging was the mode of execution for murder, burglary and robbery, and theft to the value of 12 pence or more (grand larceny) remained a capital offence visited with the customary forms of punishment. Pollock and

Maitland[8] tell us that this was burial alive at Sandwich, being thrown from the cliffs at Dover, mutilation in Winchester and, at some ports, being tied to a stake below high water and left to drown.

For petty larceny of money or goods worth less than 12 pence the punishments were whipping, the pillory or loss of an ear. For a second offence, if the ear had been lost, the second ear was now removed and for a third offence the culprit was hanged. Thus were the two different degrees of theft which had been created in 1109 still dealt with by alternative punishments that were to persist for centuries to come. Death by one means or another was the penalty for felonies subject, of course, to the criminal obtaining immunity by reading the "neck-verse," even if he learnt it after sentence of death.[9]

For treason the punishment for a man was to have his heart, bowels and entrails torn out whilst he was still alive, then to be beheaded and cut into four with the head exhibited in some public place, as happened to Sir Thomas More, as an example to others. For many a long year London Bridge was adorned with the heads of executed men fixed on poles as a warning. It was said that a traitor should perish in torments that would make hellfire seem a relief. In addition the lands of the dead man passed to the king who retained a personal interest in forfeitures.

At this time treason could be a crime against one's lord as well as the king and it was never subject to the benefit of clergy. By now all serious crimes were termed felonies, which meant cruel and wicked acts. Gradually there was taking place a transformation from largely financial compensation to capital punishment meted out by the Crown. And felonies were not only capital but also

---

8.   *Ibid.* ii. 496.
9.   Dyer. 205 pl. 6. 1561.

involved escheat of lands to the lord or to the king whose Judges heard all pleas of the Crown. A suicide forfeited his goods and chattels but not his land. He was buried at a crossroads with a stake driven through his heart, a punishment which was not mitigated until the reign of George IV. Even then he could not receive a Christian burial and still forfeited his personal estate.

The punishment of things - deodands - continued and in one case the value of a boat which caused death was given for the repair of Tewkesbury Bridge. Oxen, horses, carts, mill-wheels and cauldrons were all handed over to the king to be used to provide compensation for the victim's family or for pious or public services. Miscellaneous punishments included damages for falsely calling a woman a harlot and an offender who maliciously called someone a thief was ordered to pay damages and hold his nose with his fingers in a public parade to signify that he was a liar.

Actions for adultery, incest and bigamy could not be pursued in the lay courts as they were solely within the jurisdiction of the Church. However, for embracing the Jewish religion, for heresy and for sorcery people were sent to death by burning. In these cases, which were really ecclesiastical offences, the Church believed itself to be threatened and ironically preferred the lay courts to impose the necessary condign punishments. By the Statute of Winchester (1285) customary laws with regard to the "hue and cry" and "watch and ward" were reaffirmed and a space of 200 feet had to be cleared on each side of every highway and, within the same number of feet, no dykes were permitted to be dug in which criminals might lurk.

Trial by Jury

By *Magna Carta* (1215) it had been decreed that no free

man was to be punished except by the law of the land. As we have already observed trial by ordeal was abolished in England in 1219. The question that then arose was what should replace the ordeal. Henry III was still a boy and the Judges hesitated. In much of Europe confessions were regarded as the best proof of guilt and they were usually extracted by torture and in secret trials. In England, after some dithering, during which time many prisoners were freed or temporarily imprisoned, the Judges began to offer the accused the opportunity of having 12 men from the presenting jury determine his guilt or innocence. The need for torture was by-passed and the decision turned from the judgment of God to the conclusions of mortals.

Standing before the court the accused would be asked in what manner he would be tried. If he answered "by my country" the jury would be assembled and would reach a verdict on the basis of their own knowledge and that of their neighbours. For the first time they acted as witnesses providing information, and initially the majority would prevail. Only in 1367, in a leading case,[10] did the courts reject earlier precedents and hold that a majority verdict was void. The jury were now required to provide the same unambiguous judgment as the ordeal had done. It had nothing to do with a presumption of innocence which was a concept as yet still unknown.

If the accused, who was not permitted to call witnesses or engage counsel, refused to agree to trial by jury and stood mute when charged it was provided by the Statute of Westminster (1275) that he be kept in a hard prison, *prison forte et dure*, until he changed his mind. Justices Pateshull and Bereford, however, decided to attempt to compel prisoners to accept jury trial and changed "hard prison" into "hard pain", *peine forte et dure*.

---

10.   Y.B.Mich 41. Edw.3. 31 pl.36.

By this judgment of penance, as it was called, the prisoner was taken to an unlit dungeon where he was placed prostrate on the ground and had a heavy weight of iron or stone laid on his chest. The only food and drink he was allowed were three morsels of coarse bread on the first day, three draughts of stagnant water on the second day and so on alternately until he died. As a consequence of submitting himself to this torture he could not be tried. Those who accepted such a frightful death, rather than face trial by jury, did so to avoid their lands and goods being forfeit to the king if they were found guilty. Instead these passed to their families.

This is often claimed to be the only form of torture known in England prior to the Tudor and Stuart reigns. But mutilation was still expressly provided for in the Assizes of Clarendon and Northampton and many other punishments we have described can justly be regarded as torture. Further, according to Bracton, the most celebrated jurist of the age, men could be broken on the wheel for treason.[11] Nevertheless, the Continental practice of presuming guilt and "establishing" it with confessions extracted by torture from the guilty and innocent alike did not find acceptance here.

Juries, however, were not permitted to eat or drink, and were virtually kept prisoners, until after they had given their verdicts. And if the Judge considered a verdict to be perverse he could fine the jurors or imprison them until they changed their minds. This went some way to ensuring Crown control over juries whenever it was considered necessary but generally juries retained a good deal of independence. Nevertheless, many men went to great lengths to avoid jury service which interfered with their daily lives and was still in its infancy and not so highly regarded then as it is now.

---

11.   *De Legibus.* Lib.iii. f. 118. c.1250.

By the thirteenth century the Crown had become sufficiently strong to be able further to centralize the law at the expense of local jurisdictions. Bracton, in words that were to echo through the ages, proclaimed that, "The king is below no man, but he is below God and the law; ... the king is bound to obey the law, though if he breaks it his punishment must be left to God."[12] This was indeed defining the principle. Nevertheless, the power of the king was immense, even though in theory he was subject to chs.39 and 40 of *Magna Carta*. These provided that no free man was to be arrested, imprisoned, outlawed or banished unless by the lawful judgment of his peers, and that the king might not sell or refuse or delay right or justice. These provisions were to assume more significance later in our history, however, than in the early fourteenth century.

Rise of the Legal Profession

As royal legal jurisdiction expanded, Edward I, known as the "English Justinian" after the outstanding codifier of Roman law, needed and encouraged the growth of a legal profession. Control over the profession was given by the king to his Judges and the serjeants-at-law who were selected by the king on the recommendation of the Judges. Furthermore, only the serjeants, who as the leading counsel were originally known as servants-of-the-king, could be elevated to the bench. Their arguments and cases in court were reported in the Year Books for use as precedents and thus they "made" the common law. According to Fortescue they were the wealthiest advocates in the world.[13]

---

12. *Ibid.*
13. *De Laudibus* 124. 1470.

The ordinary lawyers were divided between pleaders (later to be called barristers) and attorneys. At this time a pleader stood next to his client in court and spoke for him, whilst an attorney represented his client who might not attend the court but would be bound by what his attorney said or agreed to on his behalf. It was from the ranks of the pleaders that serjeants were drawn and, if the king chose, they could be imprisoned for collusive or deceitful practice.

In lively courtroom scenes pleaders proved to be vigorous advocates and soon commenced the practice of citing and distinguishing earlier cases. They also played a vital role in teaching students at the four Inns of Court and the 10 lesser Inns of Chancery. As part of their education the students frequented court to listen to cases and take notes of likely precedents. They also performed their own mock trials known as "moots" and attended lectures.

Of great significance for the survival, growth and independence of the common law, in face of the revival and potential penetration of Roman law, was the fact that, unlike students at the universities, the students at the Inns of Court[14] were taught English law based to an ever-increasing extent on precedents in earlier cases. And only those called to the Bar were allowed by the Judges to practise in the courts. However, it should always be remembered that in criminal trials the accused could not have a lawyer to defend him in cases of felony - where death was the penalty.

---

14.   Coke said of the Inns that they "altogether do make the most famous universities for profession of law only, or of any human science, that is in the world, and advanceth itself above all others." *Reports.* Pref.1602.

Origin of Justices of the Peace

At the beginning of the fourteenth century, armed bands, often led by knights and clergy, roamed the countryside pillaging, murdering, taking prisoners and setting houses on fire. They were still active at the time of the Black Death (1348/9) and the Peasants' Revolt (1381) and at one point the whole of Bristol was in the hands of such a gang. There was a perceived emergency in public order and from as early as 1305 special justices, known as the Justices of Trailbaston (after the staves carried by criminals), were appointed to try these brigands, but they were generally hated for their high-handed conduct and did not last long. Nevertheless, they formed part of the transition to the "keepers of the peace".

The power of the sheriffs, who had grown over-mighty and corrupt, was by this time on the decline. In order to circumvent them the king decided to create a new commission made up of local gentry who were to be charged with keeping the peace. At first the keepers were merely required to hold prisoners in custody until they could bring them before the itinerant justices who performed the task of delivering the gaols.

By 1344, however, the keepers had acquired the authority to try and punish prisoners themselves and by the Statute of Westminster, 1361[15] they became officially Justices of the Peace, as they remain today. For most purposes the creation of the institution of the Justice of the Peace finally brought to an end the jurisdiction of the hundred and county courts, although they were not abolished until 1867. The justices became the administrative, legal and political deputies of the Crown in the counties under the direct control of the king, who appointed them, and his council.

---

15.   34 Edw.3. c.1.

Persecution of the Lollards

In 1414 the Justices of the Peace were made responsible
for suppressing the Lollards, who were followers of
Church reformer John Wycliffe. Consequently, they were
frequently indicted at the justices' Quarter Sessions. The
word "lollard" meant "idle babbler", a term of abuse used
by their enemies. Wycliffe was, however, really a
precursor of Martin Luther and Henry VIII. For instance,
he caused the Bible to be translated into English and
attacked the unseemly pursuit of wealth by the Church.
He thought Church property might properly be seized and
used for the benefit of the nation, and by proclaiming a
direct relationship between God and man he threatened
to undermine the theology of the still dominant Church
of Rome.

Nevertheless, he was a priest before his time and in
the fifteenth century his teachings provoked fear in the
hearts of the clergy and the Crown alike. As early as 1401
the Lollard William Sawtry was burned at the stake in
Smithfield Market for the heresy of teaching that "after
the consecration by the priest there remains true material
bread." Merely breaking the fast in Lent could also lead
to the stake as punishment. The "Lollards Tower" in the
Tower of london is a grim reminder of their persecution.

Although by a statute of 1401, burning was ratified as
the punishment for heresy, including for "schoolmasters
and owners of books deemed heretical," support for
Wycliffe's teachings was widespread among the common
people and even, for a time, within the ranks of the upper
classes. An illustration of the latter was Sir John
Oldcastle (Lord Cobham), and perhaps his fate was
responsible for the later loss of enthusiasm for Wycliffe
among the ranks of the wealthy.

In 1418, in the reign of Henry V, Sir John was charged
with heresy, instead of treason which was thought

unlikely to succeed. On being told by the court that if he meekly asked for absolution he could have it as a friend of the king, he responded by accusing the Archbishop of Canterbury, Thomas Arundel, who was one of his Judges, of bringing malicious and scandalous allegations against him. Again, the issue was whether there remained material bread after its consecration by a priest. Oldcastle evaded some direct questions but was found guilty of heresy by the court. He was subsequently burned to death in St Giles Field, near Temple Bar, to the accompaniment of priests cursing the crowds who had gathered to pray for him.[16]

Prior to his unfortunate end Oldcastle managed to escape from the Tower of London and call upon all Lollards to rise in defence of conscience. Thirty-seven suffered death in consequence and for the next 10 years there was a concerted persecution of Wycliffe's "Poor Priests" who, in effect, were missionaries in the mould of St Francis of Assisi. Many of them were accused of treason rather than heresy and were executed in the barbarous manner reserved for that offence. If we may venture a little into the future, however, we shall see that the issue of consecrated bread resurfaced in the reign of "Bloody Mary".

Treason

One of the first crimes to be defined by statute in medieval times was treason - the most political of all crimes. The two principal categories of treason set out in Edward III's Treason Act of 1352[17] were imagining (ie, plotting) and compassing the death of the king or levying

---

16.   *State Tryals.* iv.22.35. 1719 edn.
17.   Edw.3. st.5. c.2.

war against him. The Act required an overt deed but governments became skilled in avoiding this limitation. And treason was never clergyable. The times were dangerous and the king was still not powerful enough to prevent continuing blood-feuds, executions and arbitrary punishments among influential barons at the head of large bodies of armed retainers. They posed a constant threat to the king's peace and were deemed to be attempts to exercise royal power and thus treason. Bringing the barons into accord with the king and helping to prevent the ruin of many noble families was the political motive of the Act. A legal, and equally important, purpose was to ensure that forfeitures of land and goods following a conviction came to the king and not by way of escheat to a lord.

The statute codified and replaced the common law of treason and in doing so narrowed the scope of the crime. It also provided that any extension of its own definitions of treason should be made only by Parliament. However, with the decay of feudalism and the emergence with the Tudors of the nation state headed by an all-powerful king, the courts began to open up a fertile field of constructive extensions of the meaning of the statute as a means to exercise social control. Thus, the scope of the crime was now extensively enlarged. Certain popular activities, even including an assembly to call for higher wages, were interpreted by the Judges as tending to the destruction of the king within the meaning of the words "imagining and compassing" his death as set out in the Act. We shall come across more of this and of other statutory extensions later.

At all times until 1870 the punishment for treason was merciless. As we have already glimpsed, for a man it was to be drawn behind a cart (originally by the tail of a horse), hanged and cut down whilst still alive, disembowelled and castrated, with his intestines burnt before his eyes, and finally decapitated with the remainder of his body cut into quarters. Women, on the other hand, were burned at the stake after being tarred, although in many cases the executioner managed to strangle them before they were engulfed by the flames of the fire. Claimed to have been a remnant of Norman policy the burning of women alive was said by Blackstone in his inimitable style to be out of "the decency due to the sex (which) forbade the exposing and publicly mangling their bodies ..."[18]

That was written by Blackstone in 1769. In the same year Voltaire wrote in a commentary to Beccaria's celebrated *Crimes and Punishments:*

> Ingenious punishments to render death horrible seem rather the inventions of tyranny than of justice. In England they ripped open the belly of a man guilty of high treason; tore out his heart, dashed it in his face, and then threw it into the fire. And wherein did this high treason frequently consist? In having been, during a civil war, faithful to an unfortunate king ... At length, their manners were softened; they continued to tear out the heart, but not until after the death of the offender ...

Here we have one writer, an apologist for English law, the other more enlightened. It may be just as well for Blackstone that Voltaire did not turn his pen to the tarring and burning of women, although it must be said that in general Voltaire compared Continental penal law and torture unfavourably with that of England.

---

18.   *Comm.* iv. 78.

Other Violent Punishments

By the reign of Edward III mutilation, but not cruel punishments generally, had become unfashionable and was replaced by hanging, the pillory and the tumbrel - in descending order according to the seriousness of the crime. Imprisonment was not much used as a punishment but was by no means unknown in the grim dungeons of ancient castles, such as those at York, Exeter and Norwich, where the powerful in the land sometimes incarcerated their enemies. The King's Courts also had their own prisons including the Marshalsea of the King's Bench in Southwark, and the Fleet, off Fleet Street, which was shared by Chancery and the Star Chamber. Above all was the brooding Tower of London for the tortures decreed by the kings and their councils.

The expense of keeping prisoners was usually met by fees which the accused themselves had to pay. They were exacted when a prisoner first entered gaol, then for his food and drink whilst there, and finally on his release before he could leave gaol. If he was poor and unable to pay he would be starved, whipped and tortured.

In passing we might note an unusual statute of Edward III's by which no dinner, supper or other meal was permitted to consist of more than two courses, except on great feast days including Christmas when three might be indulged in. The mind boggles at how this might have been circumvented by a gourmand.[19] Less severe was a statute of the reign of Edward VI which provided a penalty of a fine of £10 of lawful money of England for keeping over 10 gallons of French wine in a house (7 Edw. 6, c.5).

The pillory and stocks, known from Anglo-Saxon times, were widely used in an endeavour to prevent tradesmen

---

19.   Edw.3. st.3.

falsifying weights and measures as well as against
libellous and seditious writings, prostitutes, brawlers and
common scolds. The last also suffered the tumbrel, or
ducking stool, which involved the head being fully
immersed in muddy or stinking water. The pillory
consisted of a frame of wood with moveable boards. They
contained holes through which the head and hands of the
offender, who had to stand, were placed and secured. The
stocks, on the other hand, consisted of two heavy timbers
one of which could be raised and when lowered was held
secure by a padlock. Notches in the timbers formed holes
in which the legs of the seated offender were placed and
held tightly when the timbers were closed.

A popular victim, like John Lilburne later, might be
garlanded with flowers and applauded in the pillory but
this common form of punishment for misdemeanours often
bore a close resemblance to public stoning, with the
accused defenceless before the crowd and not infrequently
stoned to death. By a statute of 1406 every village and
town in the land was required to erect a pillory for
"drunkards, gamblers and vagrants" who were often
forced to stand in it for three days at a time whilst at the
mercy of passers-by.

Flogging was another punishment for misdemeanours
such as petty theft, vagrancy, minor political offences, or
being the parent of an illegitimate child or an
unsuccessful prosecutor who could not pay costs. This
involved being tied to the tail of a cart and paraded
through the streets whilst being whipped "until the body
was bloody." A narrow street in the City of York named
"Whip-ma-Whop-ma-Gate" still bears witness to the
practice operated there, a short distance from the city
gaol.

Up to 50 lashes appears to have been the usual
sentence and it sometimes caused dumbness, mental
disorder, permanent injury and even death. Women and

children were not spared and flogging was not abolished until 1820 for women, 1948 for men and 1967 in prisons, so slowly does enlightenment about violent punishments shuffle along. Outlawry, the last resort in ancient law, still survived in the fifteenth century and in 1452 a statute of Henry VI extended this harsh punishment to rioters and disturbers of the peace - but only if they owned no land!

A form of guillotine was also in use in England, long before its invention by M. Guillotine in the French Revolution. Known as the "Halifax Gibbet" it bore a remarkable resemblance to that used in the French Terror and was mentioned in *Holinshed's Chronicle* in 1587. Between 1541 and 1650 49 people were executed in Halifax by means of the Gibbet.

In Scotland a similar machine, known there as "The Maiden", was introduced by the Earl of Morton in 1565 and was used to behead him in 1587, after he had been Regent of Scotland for 10 years. The Earl of Argyle, when laying his head upon it, called it "a sweet maiden, whose embrace would waft his soul into heaven."[20] Hence its otherwise incongruous nickname. Its use was discontinued in 1710 but it may still be seen in the Museum of Antiquaries of Scotland in Edinburgh.

Sanctuary and abjuration of the realm existed in remote ages and pre-dated Christianity. They resurfaced in the laws of Ine (c.5), Alfred (c.5), Athelstan (iv.4) and Ethelred (vii.5) when the Church did not want religious places profaned by the use of force. Three and five days appear to have been the maximum periods of grace in Anglo-Saxon laws but by the fourteenth century sanctuary was generally permitted for 40 days. During this time fleeing criminals, including murderers, were granted immunity from the long arm of the law, and even the

---

20.   Wm. Andres: *Bygone Punishments*. 121. 1931 edn.

reach of the king.

During sanctuary, however, the fugitive had to decide whether to give himself up for trial or abjure the realm. Abjuration meant leaving the country on foot by a prescribed route to a named port. If he deviated from the route, or took longer than the time allotted to him, he could be killed on the spot by a revenge-seeker. Even if he succeeded in getting abroad his goods were estreated, his lands forfeited and his wife treated as a widow. Nevertheless, some powerful religious houses, such as Durham and Beverley, were prepared to grant permanent sanctuary. Henry VIII later described sanctuaries as "dens of thieves" and when he reformed the Church he destroyed most sanctuaries and the remainder, with a few exceptions, were finally abolished in 1623.

Corruption to Stability

Appointing commissions was a favourite device of medieval kings and Edward III used one to investigate corruption amongst Judges, barons, sheriffs and office-holders generally. Serious corruption of Judges was exposed and many were dismissed from the Bench. Henceforth, Judges had to take an oath to administer true justice and take no bribes or gifts. Lawyers too were shown to have taken fees from both parties in cases in which they were involved. The Chief Justice of England, William Thorpe, was convicted on five counts of bribery and was sentenced to be hanged, although the king intervened to reprieve him.

The pillory continued to be in great demand also as a punishment for tradesmen giving short weight, or selling bad food and false jewellery, as well as for fortune-tellers and petty pilferers. Sometimes less dangerous and more imaginative punishments might be imposed. A fishmonger selling bad fish, for example, could be paraded through the streets with a collar of stinking fish over his shoulders. A baker selling short-weight loaves might be perambulated with loaves of bread around his neck, and a drunkard paraded in a barrel with his head protruding from the top and his hands from holes in the sides.

It is not surprising that during the distress and disorder occasioned by the Wars of the Roses in the second half of the fifteenth century violence increased, corruption continued to spread and the common law began to stagnate and fall into disrepute. Jurors were no longer required to be witnesses and in consequence of an increase in independent sources of evidence the influence of the then more flexible Court of Chancery grew, and the Star Chamber began to emerge in an effort to bring about changes in, and prestige to, the law.

Among the war-weary population the desire for law and order, as well as justice, was also coming to the fore once again. After the battle of Bosworth in 1485 the victorious new Tudor king, Henry VII, began the task of stabilizing the country. It was to Henry VIII, however, that the role of generating a substantial change in the administration of the law and punishments fell.

CHAPTER 4

ROYAL POWER

Political Control

With the strong central government of the Tudors came
an increase in the severity of the penal law. The rise of
the nation state meant that once again political struggles
expressed themselves in the language of the law. First,
in the preamble to the statute 4 Henry VII, c.13 (1489),
the king deplored that many people who could read had
come to rely upon the privilege of clergy to be bold in
committing murder, rape, robbery and theft. In response,
the Act provided that those not actually in holy orders
who had once benefited from their "clergy" should not be
able to do so twice.

Accordingly, murderers obtaining immunity from
execution were to have branded on their left thumb with
a hot iron the letter "M" and thieves a "T". Accessories,
however, were to be hanged for their principal's first
offence which seems somewhat illogical. Sir James
Fitzjames Stephen was to comment on the statute that
until this time, "anyone who could read might commit
murder as often as he pleased, with no other result than
that of being delivered to the Ordinary to make his

purgation."[1] Clearly the king was not prepared to countenance the full effects of the farce any longer, but benefit of clergy still continued and saved as many as two in five murderers and thieves from death.

By the time Henry VIII came to the throne in 1509 the foundations of the state were secure. Yet Henry set about wielding unprecedented arbitrary power over the council, Parliament and the courts. Nevertheless, he was careful always to act within the letter of the law although he often had it changed to suit his purpose. Even when he had replaced the Pope as Head of the Church of England, and provided that to speak, publish or hold a view to the contrary was heresy to be punished by burning at the stake, he did so by statute.[2]

No doubt Henry felt some insecurity following his breach with Rome, and he notoriously extended the law of treason as a means of political control, although, again, by "due process" through Parliament and the courts. All political opposition was to be suppressed, however weak and flimsy. Men were executed for high treason even when engaged solely in outbursts against enclosures of land, or against Catholics, religious meeting places and brothels, or simply meeting to press for higher wages.

The uttering of mere words was made treason by 26 Hen. VIII, c.13 which, at the same time widening the scope of the offence, enacted that "to wish, will or desire by words or writing ... any bodily harm to the King, Queen or their heirs" was sufficient. And, an intention not to kill, but to put any kind of restraint by force upon the king was held by the courts to be evidence of an intention to destroy him, and that included assemblies with no true political content whatsoever.[3] In one case the rack was

---

1.   *Op. cit.* i. 463.
2.   31 Hen.8. c.14. 1539.
3.   Coke. *3 Inst.* 12.

used on a John Archer to get him to reveal the names of his "treasonable" companions in rioting.

Treason by words alone may, in fact, have existed at common law since Sir Matthew Hale quoted a case from the time of Edward IV where a certain "Walter Walker, dwelling at the sign of the *Crown* in Cheapside, told his little child, if he would be quiet, he would make him heir of the Crown." For that he was adjudged guilty of treason in speaking disrespectfully of the king.[4] However, Henry's Act was meant to leave no one in any doubt.

It was endorsed in *R. v. Owen*,[5] by Coke himself when he decided that it was treason by "open deed" to say that the king, being excommunicated by the Pope, might lawfully be deposed and killed. Yet, later, in his Third Institute Coke was to say that "bare words may make a heretick, but not a traytor without an overt act."[6] Clearly at the time of *Owen* he thought such bare words should themselves be construed as an act if they even remotely might conceivably lead to the death of the king and possibly threaten the Reformation itself.

Henry VIII's high-handed extension of the treason law is also illustrated in regard to the crime of poisoning. In 1531 Richard Rouse, a cook in the household of Bishop Fisher, was accused of attempting to poison his master. Henry had a statute enacted[7] to attaint him of high treason with a punishment of boiling to death in hot water. According to Coke a young woman named Margaret Davy was also boiled to death in Smithfield, for the "poysoning of her mistris" and some others suffered the same fate.

Odious though poisoning is, the Act and its punishment

---

4.   Hale. *P.C.* i. 115.
5.   1 Rolle Rep. 185. (1616).
6.   *Op. cit.* 14.
7.   22 Hen.8, c.9.

were widely considered to be too severe, and the offence too remote from treason to the king, with the result that it was replaced immediately Mary came to the throne. Nevertheless, in regard to treason Henry undoubtedly unleashed a reign of terror which was to continue under Elizabeth. And despite the above-mentioned repeal, "Bloody Mary" used the heresy laws in place of treason to cause some 300 Protestants, including women and children, to burn at the stake in her vain attempt to restore the Catholic religion.

Mary reversed her father's religious laws and submitted herself and the country to Rome. Whether bread remained after consecration was still in issue and the principal Protestant "heretics", Archbishop Cranmer and Bishops Latimer and Ridley, were incarcerated in the Tower. From there they were taken to Oxford in an attempt to persuade them to the Catholic view in dispute with learned men. As the sages failed to convince, Mary soon had Latimer and Ridley burnt at Oxford, having strained mercy by having bags of gunpowder strung around their necks to hasten death. Notwithstanding, they died in terrible pain with Latimer crying out his immortal words: "Play the man, Master Ridley; and we shall this day light such a candle by God's grace in England as I trust shall never be put out." Cranmer was sent to the stake later since special permission was required from Rome to burn an archbishop.

Demons

Witchcraft, sorcery and "unnatural love" were made crimes by statute for the first time in 1542 although they had been punishable as far back as Anglo-Saxon times. This Act also was repealed when Mary came to the throne in 1547 but was revived by another in 1563. The offences were non-clergyable and by the new Act hanging or burning became the penalty for witchcraft, enchantment, charm or sorcery provided a person was killed or destroyed as a result. At common law, death remained the punishment for a second offence even if no one was killed.

It might appear that the proviso would make the statute a dead letter but as such offences were virtually unprovable, suspicion alone was accepted by the courts as sufficient to uphold an accusation. This was particularly so if the accused bore a mark of the devil on her body - usually any birthmark or flea-bite would do. Even strong smells in a house might be held to be sufficient "proof" since it was widely believed that those in thrall to the devil kept imps in pots and other vessels which smelt "detestably". Also, using ointment which an informer alleged was made from the fat of children dug out of their graves could be enough to brand a woman as a witch. Absence of the accused from the scene of witchcraft provided no alibi and even young children were accepted as competent "witnesses" for the prosecution.

This is another crime that we shall see grow and fester, particularly when the witch-hunting was encouraged by the demonologist James I who wrote a book against the "detestable slaves of the devil" called, not surprisingly, *Demonologie*. Apparently James had felt himself aggrieved by witches detaining him with contrary winds when he undertook a romantic visit to Denmark in search of a queen. Under the Stuarts women were tortured to make them confess to witchcraft often with the "witches' bridle", an iron collar with a metal gag clamped around the neck and jaw which was slowly tightened. Immediately after his succession to the throne of England James secured a statute, 1 Jac.1, c.12, 1603, to strengthen this obnoxious law which was so dear to his heart.

All this time every accused person in a criminal trial

was the victim of severe injustice in the sphere of procedure. Once arrested he was held in secure confinement without being told the nature of the evidence against him, or the identity of any witnesses the prosecution proposed to call. He was not allowed any facilities for preparing his defence and at the trial there were no rules of evidence. He was not permitted to call witnesses himself, so no alibi could be proved and, as we have seen, in cases of felony he could not engage counsel to defend him although his very life was at risk. Confessions of accomplices were particularly welcomed against him.

All this was based on the spurious argument that the Judge would take the part of the accused, which Coke accepted in his Third Institute.[8] Even if this were likely - which it was not - the long and tiring hearings of the time would have made it difficult and, in any event, when the Crown wanted to, it could choose both the Judge and the members of the jury. Also, since jurymen by now were less likely to be witnesses, written depositions from others were accepted and Judges became more powerful *vis-à-vis* the jury.

Furthermore, Judges and juries had to hear a case through to its end without a break and the jury were still denied all food and drink until they had reached a verdict. Bribery of juries was also only too common and if the Judge, or the Star Chamber, considered their verdict was perverse the jurors could still be fined and imprisoned. For instance, when Sir Nicholas Throgmorton was found not guilty of treason in 1554 the jury were bound over in a sum of £500 each to answer for their verdict and were told by Lord Chief Justice Bromley, "Take good care what you do." The answer they all gave in this case was, "Let

---

8.   *Op. cit.* 29.

us not be molested for discharging our consciences truly,"[9] but not all jurors were so brave.

The less serious offences were dealt with by the Justices of the Peace who could themselves impose severe punishments, including imprisonment, in the secrecy of their own homes. An improvement occurred, however, when, where an accused was to be sent for trial to a higher court, justices were required by two statutes[10] in Mary's reign to hold a preliminary investigation of the prisoner and any witnesses and to reduce to writing all the material evidence. Witnesses could also now be bound over to appear at the trial.

Prior to that, justices were given a particularly unpleasant role to play by Henry VIII and his son Edward. Henry's dissolution of the monasteries and other large ecclesiastical properties had created a huge roaming population of vagrants including out-of-work labourers. These were now to be harried from pillar to post and worse.

Following his father's example Edward VI enacted[11] that they should be branded with the letter "V" to identify them. Additionally, such a man was to be made a slave for two years to the person who had informed on him, with the statute additionally providing that he could be beaten, and chained with a ring round his neck, arm or leg. If he managed to run away but was caught he was to be branded on the face with an "S" and enslaved for life. If he escaped a second time he was to be executed.

Torture

The principal effects of the Reformation were to

---

9. *State Tryals. Op. cit.* iv. 47.
10. 1, 2 Philip & Mary c.13. 1554 and 3 Philip & Mary c.10. 1555.
11. 1 Edw.6. c.3.

subordinate the Church to the state, to increase royal revenues and to enable Henry VIII to secure the support of the barons with timely gifts of Church lands. In turn, this enhanced the growing influence of the Council of State which became transformed into the Court of Star Chamber. A separate Privy Council was then promoted which attended the king personally. The common law was allowed to stagnate at a time when sovereign government desired cogent criminal laws to ensure that the king's will was enforced.

The Star Chamber filled that role. It could not impose the death penalty for felonies but it established a wide and efficient jurisdiction, particularly over offences affecting public order and the security of the state. At first it was generally welcomed, not least by Coke, as forcing the will of the law (and of the king) on the wealthy who in the past had often been able to secure immunity at a price. It became infamous, however, for its arbitrary procedures and its use of torture.

Clause 39 of Magna Carta forbade torture and on the trial of John Felton, who had assassinated the Duke of Buckingham at Portsmouth in 1628, all the 12 Judges sitting at Serjeant's Inn declared unanimously that no man should be tortured on the rack since, "no such punishment is known or allowed at common law." That clearly indicates that the Judges knew of the existence of the rack and of the use of torture by royal prerogative. And, Coke added his voice by proclaiming, "there is no law to warrant tortures in this land nor can they ever be justified."[12]

Notwithstanding these unambiguous statements from the judiciary torture continued to be used extensively by the Star Chamber to secure confessions and persuade prisoners to implicate others. This was torture practised

---

12.   *Op. cit.*

outside the law by the political rulers of the country as a means to protect their political control. As Blackstone was to comment, the rack was "an engine of the state not of law." The well-known martyr Edmund Campion was only one of the Jesuit priests whose mere presence in England was made a crime and who were imprisoned in the Tower of London on charges of having correspondence with foreign powers. There they were subjected to the most appalling tortures before being executed.

Indeed, under Elizabeth alone 187 priests are said to have been put to death after suffering torture. And the queen was usually directly involved in the decision. For example, in 1571, in authorizing the torture of two servants of the Duke of Norfolk, the queen wrote, "We warrant you to cause them both, or either of them, to be brought to the rack ... and to find the taste thereof."

With all the Tudor monarchs the rack was in constant use in the Tower. According to Sir Matthew Hale it was used on charges of "accroaching of royal power" which he described as a "very uncertain charge, that no man could well tell what defence to make to it."[13] It has often been suggested that the royal prerogative was to blame when torture took place. And indeed it was in the sense that it was all the excuse the Star Chamber needed but it must not be forgotten that specific instructions from either the monarch or the council were always required before the torturer could act.

David Jardine, a nineteenth century barrister and writer on historical and legal matters, was to expose the vast cover-up of the operation of torture in the Tudor and Stuart reigns with his *Reading on Torture*.[14] Jardine's

---

13.   *Op. cit.* i. 80.
14.   *A Reading on the Use of Torture in the Criminal Law of England prior to the Commonwealth.* Delivered at New Inn Hall, Michaelmas Term, 1836. Reprinted in the *Edinburgh Review.* vol.67 (April-July 1838).

researches into the Registers of the Proceedings of the
council and original torture warrants of the State Papers
Office revealed the extensive use of the rack for
dislocating limbs in order to persuade victims to "confess"
to treason, murder or robbery. Letters from the successive
monarchs, including Elizabeth, and the council were
discovered which instructed the Lieutenant of the Tower
to use torture. And instruments such as the hideous
"Scavenger's Daughter" which painfully used iron hoops
and manacles to tie the neck and feet together were
revealed as an ordinary part of the tortures wielded by
the Crown and the Star Chamber.

Similarly, an iron gauntlet compressed by a screw, a
spiked collar known as "the necklace", thumb screws and
putting the prisoner in a rat-infested dungeon were
employed frequently. For instance, in 1577, accused of
hearing mass, Thomas Sherwood was placed in a Tower
dungeon below high-water mark. Water flowed in and out
with the tides bringing with it rats which tore the flesh
from his arms and legs. He was then put to the rack.
Despite such cruelty he admitted nothing and was
executed for high treason.

Torture in its narrow sense meant its use to extract a
confession or evidence against others. But William
Prynne, a barrister of Lincoln's Inn, might be forgiven for
thinking that his open punishment bore a strong
resemblance to torture in a more general sense. As a
Puritan he wrote a book in 1633 called *Histriomastix*
which contained critical references to stage plays,
comedies, masques, dancing, bonfires and maypoles.
Despite Prynne's sincere motives it was not a very
uplifting book. But what of its consequences? The charge
against Prynne of high treason for writing this book
complained that he well knew that the Queen Henrietta
was sometimes a spectator at such masques and dances
at court.

For thus offending the majesty of Charles I's consort, Prynne was fined £500, placed in the pillory, burned on the forehead, had both his ears cut off and was imprisoned in the Tower for life. As one of the Judges of the Court of Star Chamber, the Chancellor of the Exchequer said that the punishment was a mercy as men had been hanged and quartered for far less. The Lord Chief Justice added that his heart swelled and the blood in his veins boiled to see this attempted which might endanger the sovereign. In giving their ferocious sentence the Judges, who were beside themselves with rage, added the Prynne should never be set at liberty since he was a mad dog not fit to live in a den with such monsters as wolves and tigers like himself.[15]

Prynne, who never gave up, was to be punished again later, but many others lost their heads first time round. These included three of the wives of Henry VIII, Thomas More, Mary Queen of Scots, Sir Walter Raleigh, Lord Strafford and Archbishop Laud. It seemed that no one was safe. Indeed, as well as the famous, John Stowe, in his *Survey of London* published in the year of the accession to the throne of James I, claimed that 72,000 persons had been hanged in the reign of Henry VIII alone. It is not easy to judge how accurate this figure is but the number was undoubtedly very high.

The Star Chamber

As we have seen, the Star Chamber was the king's council sitting as a prerogative court. This meant that it wielded immense powers in attempting to substitute the will of the sovereign for the common law. It was composed of the Lord Chancellor, the Chief Justices of the King's Bench

---

15.   *State Tryals. Op. cit.* 273.

and the Common Pleas and privy councillors. The presence of the senior Judges of the realm at its hearings came from it originally being perceived as ancillary to the common law courts, and in its early life it was indeed highly regarded as a body that dispensed justice with speed and flexibility. It punished conspiracy, false accusations, riots, forgery, bribery and intimidation, often bringing to book the powerful, who were used to evading the law.

It also had the dangerous power to admonish "wayward" county justices and to punish juries with whose verdicts it did not agree. Additionally, it kept a close eye on the publication of libels and the newly invented printing of books. It came into existence to check abuses but as a prerogative court acting on behalf of powerful monarchs it gradually became an instrument of arbitrary rule, even evading writs of habeas corpus issued by the common-law courts. This brought no outraged response since the Judges were appointed by the king and subservient to him. Its political role was to deal, usually with brutality, with offenders it considered likely to imperil the authority of the state.

After a time the Star Chamber made itself feared and hated as a ruthless arm of royal power transcending the common law. It came more and more to rely uncritically on unscrupulous informers and, as we have seen, to use torture and harsh punishments without regard to the consequences. For instance, in February 1637 John Lilburne, or "Freeborn John" as he was affectionately known, was charged with distributing religious literature which the Star Chamber had banned.

He refused to take the self-incriminating *ex-officio* oath, thus giving birth to the accused's right of silence. For this refusal he was fined £500 and savagely whipped along the entire route from the Fleet prison, next to Fleet Street, to Westminster where, bloody but unbowed, he was forced into the pillory. Here he was garlanded with flowers by a large crowd who had gathered and who demanded a speech from their hero. Defiantly, and in great physical distress with open weals on his back "bigger than tobacco pipes," he managed to comply. As a consequence, by order of the council he was gagged so brutally that his mouth bled profusely.

On being returned to the Fleet, Lilburne was confined in isolation, denied medical assistance and refused food, water and bedding. He would undoubtedly have starved to death if friends had not managed surreptitiously to reach him with food and drink. He later stated that he had been treated with an "abundance of inhuman, barbarous cruelty," which was no exaggeration since he was kept in irons and, although ill for 11 months, sometimes with a fever, he was constantly kicked and beaten.

Notwithstanding all of this, he never recanted or took the *ex-officio* oath and remained in prison until released by the Long Parliament. On May 4, 1641 Parliament resolved that the sentence of the Star Chamber on Lilburne was illegal, and "bloody, wicked, cruel, barbarous and tyrannical." In consequence it awarded him compensation of £3,000, but he saw little of it.[16] Nevertheless, he went on to become an important figure in the Commonwealth as leader of the influential Levellers. But this did not give him immunity from a further state trial as we shall see.

The Star Chamber was not a court of record. This did not inhibit it, however, from enlarging the criminal law and constantly imposing crippling fines and imprisonment for life despite Coke's view that only a court of record had such jurisdiction.[17] At this stage Coke was ignored and

---

16.   *State Trials.* 1735 edn. vol.7. 260.
17.   2 *Inst.* 71: 4 *Inst.* 135.

the Star Chamber continued to inflict cruel punishments and torture on all whom it saw as political opponents of the monarch. Apart from tortures in the Tower, the following were all used to terrorize the people, viz., whipping, branding, cutting off ears, the pillory, slitting of noses and being tied in a sack and flung to the dogs.

Such punishments were entirely at the whim of the Judges of the Chamber who were wholly unrestrained by a jury, or statutory or common-law authority. They examined in private those brought before them as witnesses and their primary rationale was not to inquire into guilt or innocence but, however unjustly, to uphold royal absolutism.

Another prerogative court, and one which worked closely with the Star Chamber, was the ecclesiastical High Commission, created by Elizabeth both to guard public morals and to maintain the royal supremacy. An example of both functions operating in tandem is furnished by *Traske's Case* (1618) where a Jew observing the Jewish Sabbath and avoiding pork was sentenced for opinions tending to sedition and commotion and scandalizing the king and the bishops.

The Commission re-opened old scars in its disputes with the common-law Judges, of whom Coke was the most active in issuing prohibitions against its judgments. Its procedures too aroused fierce passions with Puritans claiming that it was tyrannical, brutal and oppressive; an enemy of liberty and truth.

As with the Star Chamber a person accused before it had to take the *ex-officio* oath which in effect required him to convict himself by confessing to an accusation of an unspecified crime levelled by an undisclosed informer. A refusal was treated as a plea of guilty and the hapless prisoner was handed over to the Star Chamber for punishment. Using the Commission as a weapon Archbishop Whitgift's campaign against Puritans was likened to the Spanish Inquisition. It comes as no surprise then that when Charles I was obliged to call the Long Parliament in 1640 it promptly abolished both the Star Chamber and the High Commission, as well as other prerogative courts, and brought torture to a end. The Star Chamber, it declared, had been a means to introduce arbitrary power and government.

Common-law Punishments

Nevertheless, during this period even the common-law courts had remained busy dispensing the death penalty. Stephen claimed that there were some 800 executions in the year 1598 alone[18] and Coke at the conclusion of his Third Institute was to write:

> What a lamentable case it is to see so many Christian men and women strangled on that cursed tree of the gallows, insomuch as if in a large field a man might see together all the Christians that but in one year, throughout England come to that untimely and ignominious death, if there were any spark of grace, or charity in him, it would make his heart bleed for pity and compassion ... True it is that we have found by woeful experience, that it is not frequent and often punishment that does prevent like offences ... Those offences are often committed that are often punished: for the frequency of the punishment makes it so familiar as it is not feared.[19]

Not until the nineteenth century was Coke's compassion taken seriously.

The career of Sir Edward Coke (1552-1634) is certainly

---

18. *Op. cit.* i. 468.
19. *Op. cit.* Epilogue.

revealing. In a series of notable state trials he first gave great service to the Tudor Crown. But he considered the common law to be well-nigh perfect, with the Judges (and the king) subject to it. James I, on the contrary, believed that the royal prerogative was superior to the law and that the Judges were his civil servants. The strong reigns of Henry VIII and Elizabeth had given James a false sense of security. Accepting the doctrine of the "divine right of kings" he began to abuse his power without the caution of his predecessors.

Of all the Judges only Coke was prepared to do battle with the king, however, and ultimately he became leader of the parliamentary opposition to the Crown and sponsor of the Petition of Right which made forced loans to the king illegal and provided that no free man should be imprisoned or detained without cause shown. Coke also did a great deal in his judgments and writings to refashion the common law, whilst claiming only to be re-stating it, to suit the needs of the new and expanding society.

To return to the common law, the distinction between murder and manslaughter, then called "chance medley," was by now established, with malice aforethought as a required essential ingredient for the former which had become non-clergyable. Intent to kill, however, was still not necessary. On the other hand, provocation could reduce murder to manslaughter, but not if it consisted merely of words. And, as with verbal provocation, where a man grimaced at another who responded by killing him it was murder.[20] Swords were commonly worn and often used so that in 1604 the Stabbing Act[21] made stabbing murder, provided the man had not struck first and that he died within six months. At this time also sodomy,

---

20.   *Brain's Case.* (1600). Cro. Eliz. 778.
21.   2 Jac.1. c.8.

bigamy and the violation of a girl under 10 years of age were made felonies punishable with death.

A statute of Henry VII[22] had anticipated the notorious Waltham Black Act of 1723, of which more later, by making it a felony to hunt in the night, or at any time with painted faces, in any forest, park or warren. The motives for the Act, unlike those for the Black Act which were personal to Sir Robert Walpole and his friends in their pursuit of power, were a fear that assembling for hunting and sport gave opportunities for riot and disorder, and a belief that these activities should be the privilege of landowners, whilst other classes kept to their proper stations in life.

At all events Coke described the Act as "this new and ill-planned law" and demanded that it be construed strictly.[23] Although by the reign of Elizabeth, the Act had become a dead letter, in the meantime the thrust of its provision had been extended by Henry VIII with a statute[24] making it a crime punishable by death to fish in a private pond by night or break the head of a private pond by either night or day. Alongside such enactments the general Game Laws were also strengthened during this period.

Sorcery, or making a compact with the devil, was transferred from the exclusive jurisdiction of the ecclesiastical courts to be dealt with as a felony at common law. Maitland described sorcery as "a crime created by the measures taken for its suppression"[25] which would apply with equal force to witchcraft, conjuring and other such "criminal" activities. Witches were not only executed but first had to suffer a

---

22.   1 Hen.7. c.7-8. (1485).
23.   *Op. cit.* c.21. 74-7.
24.   31 Hen.8. c.2. 1539.
25.   *Op. cit.* ii. 554.

particularly unpleasant torture known as a "waking".

For this an iron hoop would be bound across the face of the unfortunate victim with four prongs thrust into her mouth. She was then bound to a wall with chains in such a manner that she could only stand. She was kept in this position for several days with relays of men present to ensure that she did not sleep. During this agonizing time long pins were inserted into her body in an effort to discover painless spots that would prove her bargain with the devil. Gypsies who refused to leave the country were declared felons, and swearing, cursing, drunkenness and profaning the Lord's day were made penal misdemeanours.

The period also witnessed an attempt to distinguish between paupers who were genuinely poor and those who were poor because they were idle and lazy. Elizabeth's famous Poor Law Act of 1601 provided for relief for the former, to be paid from local rates imposed on householders and landowners. In contrast, for the allegedly poor and idle, her brother, Edward VI, had presented London with the House of Bridewell in 1553 to set them to work rather than solely to imprison them. This was followed, in 1576, with another statute[26] of Elizabeth requiring Justices of the Peace in Quarter Sessions to set up in the counties Houses of Correction (later known as "Bridewells") in order to punish vagrants but also to set them to work. This was the first serious attempt to use labour as a reformative aspect to punishment and it laid the basis for the later retreat from the ubiquitous death penalty and the rise of the penitentiary.

Presumably not all of the poor could be hounded all of the time. As the Bridewells were not simply gaols, the able-bodied were put to productive work with the aim of

---

26.   18 Eliz. c.3.

correcting their "unacceptable" behaviour. Only with the Gaol Act of 1823 were these institutions incorporated with the county gaols to become prisons, although still under the control of Quarter Sessions.

Nevertheless, however desirable "correction" may have seemed to the legislature, at all times the paramount need was perceived to be to keep order. Hence, adhering closely to Edward VI's earlier statute enslaving the out-of-work, an Act of 1572[27] claimed that the country was infested with vagabonds who were daily responsible for horrible murders, thefts and other great outrages. On that premise it provided that all able-bodied vagrants over 14 years of age should be seized, prosecuted, whipped and burnt through the right ear. After that they would be immune from further seizure for 40 days but if after that time they were still vagrants they were to be put to death.

It is clear from all that has been said here that, compared with medieval times, the reigns of the Tudors and early Stuarts saw a substantial increase in the range of the severity of the criminal law and punishments in order to reinforce the coercive power of the Crown. So far as the common law is concerned, we can only agree with the words of Professor Milsom that, by the sixteenth century, in criminal matters it had done "no more than systematize barbarity."[28]

---

27.   14 Eliz. c.5.
28.   *Historical Foundations of the Common Law.* 361. 1969 edn.

CHAPTER 5

THE COMMONWEALTH

Penal Law Reform (1649-1660)[1]

As we have seen under the reigns last referred to, the Crown had assumed a large discretionary power to imprison and torture its subjects. The great advantage the Commonwealth inherited lay in the abolition of the prerogative courts by the Long Parliament in 1641. Their unlawful powers and procedures were now out of the way and Cromwell was inclined to proceed further with significant reforms of the criminal (and civil) law. In the first Protectorate Parliament, in 1654, he promised to reform the laws by making them plain, short and less expensive. Then, on September 17, 1656, he told the second Protectorate Parliament, "... there are wicked and abominable laws that will be in your power to alter."[2] Nevertheless, Cromwell was not about to change the coercive *nature* of the law.

Earlier, in 1652, the Rump Parliament had established the Hale Commission, composed of both lawyers and

---

1. An excellent study of this period is to be found in Donald Veall, *The Popular Movement for Law Reform 1640-1660.* 1970.
2. W.C. Abbott, ed. *The Writings and Speeches of Oliver Cromwell.* iv. 27. 1937-47.

laymen, to consider law reform under the chairmanship of Sir Matthew Hale. Hale was a skilful advocate who had acted as adviser to Lord Stafford in 1640 and as counsel for Archbishop Laud on his impeachment in 1643. A Member of Parliament and a Judge of the Common Pleas during the Commonwealth, Hale was made Chief Baron of the Exchequer at the Restoration and became Chief Justice of the King's Bench in 1671. Cromwell is said to have persuaded Hale to support him with the argument that if he was not to be permitted to govern by red gowns, he was resolved to govern by red coats.

Hale's contemporary reputation was of a man of great personal and intellectual honesty and an outstanding advocate, jurist, Judge and law reformer. Roger North said of him, "both gentle and simple, lawyers and laymen, idolise him as if there had never been such a miracle of justice since Adam."[3] More recently, legal historian Sir William Holdsworth regarded Hale as the first of our great modern lawyers and said of his work, *The Amendment or Alteration of the Lawes*, that "no wiser tract on this topic has ever been written in the whole course of the history of English law."[4] However, Andrew Amos, one of the 1833 Criminal Law Commissioners, took a less sanguine view of Hale which appears to have escaped general notice.[5]

The Hale Commission was conservative in some of its proposed revisions of the law but in others it anticipated humanitarian reform by over a century and a half. It called, for example, for the abolition of the benefit of clergy which was not achieved until 1827. For perjury, on the other hand, which had a religious dimension the

---

3.   *Life of the Late Lord Keeper Guilford.* 64. 1742.
4.   "Sir Matthew Hale." 156 *LQR* (October 1923) 422.
5.   *Ruins of Time Exemplified in Sir Matthew Hale's History of the Pleas of the Crown.* 1856.

Commission proposed the pillory, loss of ears, the slitting of the nostrils, searing with a hot iron and six months in a House of Correction, drastic punishments indeed, although short of the death penalty previously imposed. Otherwise, only for grand larceny did the Commission recommend the abolition of capital punishment, although that in itself was a large step forward.

Some reformers wanted to see the death penalty abolished only for petty theft, whilst those who wanted it ended altogether for stealing argued that it was an invitation to murder witnesses to prevent them giving evidence. In the event, for theft to the value of 12 pence or more (grand larceny) the Commission proposed that the thief be burnt on the left hand and be forced to undergo hard labour until he could pay compensation of treble the worth of the property stolen to the victim.

They also recommended that prisoners should be permitted to engage counsel in all cases where the prosecution was represented. This was not achieved until 1836 with the Prisoners Counsel Act and the Commissioners did not endear themselves to the legal profession by insisting that counsel should not receive a fee in excess of £5 for any one case. John Lilburne, for his part, was anxious to see the country rid of "vermin and caterpillars" as he described the lawyers. This has not, however, been an unusual demand by radicals throughout the centuries.

It is interesting to note that even under the new regime, which was now endeavouring as hard as any king to consolidate its power, the perpetual rebel Lilburne was again before the courts. In October 1649 he was charged before an extraordinary Commission of Oyer and Terminer with high treason for publishing among other things the Levellers' blueprint for democracy, *An Agreement of the People*.

By now a Lieutenant-Colonel in the parliamentary

army, Lilburne immediately claimed from the Judges the "liberty of every free-born Englishman namely the benefit of the laws." Given more leeway than he had ever received at the hands of the Star Chamber he constantly out-talked the Judges and when two of them whispered together he claimed that to do so was against the liberties of Englishmen. When they replied that it was nothing to his detriment he did not hesitate to reply that there was no way he could know that.

He invoked Coke, "that great Oracle of the Laws of England," and objected violently against the denial to him of counsel when his life was at risk - a right not granted in treason trials until 1695. When the jury found him not guilty of any of the alleged treasons they were themselves taken to the Old Bailey to be examined. However, they all avowed that they had only discharged their consciences, whereupon they were set free.

Lilburne had demanded that his trial be held in public and on his acquittal the acclamation of the crowds in the courtroom caused pandemonium for half an hour with the Judges "pale and hanging their heads." Amidst wild jubilation bonfires were lit throughout London but the government continued to detain Lilburne in prison until they could no longer withstand the public clamour for his release.[6]

Generally speaking, the reformers desired to mitigate the inhumanity of the penal laws but they had some strange ways of going about it. For example, *peine forte et dure* was to be abolished but standing mute was to be treated as a plea of guilty and deemed a conviction. The plea of "not guilty" was dispensed with and replaced with "I abide my lawful trial" which can hardly be counted an improvement. More positive was the decision that women felons would be hanged instead of being burned alive at

---

6.   *State Tryals. Op. cit.* 580.

the stake.

Forfeiture for suicide was abolished and the reformers proposed the abolition of all forfeitures as causing unjust hardship to the offender's wife and children, a hardship deplored in the eighteenth century by Sir Samuel Romilly as being a consequence of all executions. In place of forfeiture the Puritans would have provided for compensation, whipping and forced labour as alternative punishments. The Levellers wanted to see a salaried prison service with prisoners treated humanely at public expense. Curiously, however, for offences involving violence they favoured punishment by analogy with an eye for an eye, a limb for a limb and a life for a life.

The abolition of the criminal jurisdiction of the ecclesiastical courts in 1641 had largely brought an end to the age-old religious persecution for sexual offences. However, in 1650 an Act was passed by the Rump Parliament which made adultery a felony without benefit of clergy. This applied to married women who committed what was now a crime but not to married men. Nevertheless, since the penalty was death, juries were reluctant to convict, even when the evidence was conclusive, and only three women were executed before the statute fell into disuse after the Restoration.

As this indicates not all was sweetness and light and the case of James Nayler illustrates the harshness of Puritan thinking on so-called offences proscribed by their own religious dogmas. Nayler, a Quaker, was an eloquent preacher who, in October 1656, seated on an ass, re-enacted at Bristol Christ's entry into Jerusalem. The House of Commons decided to investigate this "blasphemy". One MP testified that he had, "often been troubled in my thoughts to think of this toleration."[7] Against the wishes of Cromwell, the Commons

---

7.   J.T. Rutt. ed. *The Diary of Thomas Burton Esq.* i. 24. 1889.

hysterically denounced Quakers and sentenced the harmless and bewildered Nayler to branding on the forehead with the letter "B", mutilation of his tongue with a hot iron, standing in the pillory, flogging twice, and indefinite imprisonment which in the event lasted three years before he was released.[8]

In the end the Protectorate produced little by way of reform of the penal law. In part, this was because it did not survive long enough, and also because its proposals gave rise to strong opposition from the wealthy and the majority of the legal profession, both of whom felt threatened by the law being made less severe. Nonetheless, even the negative results proved to be significant. The procedures and tortures of the Star Chamber were never restored, the common law re-established its supremacy and although ecclesiastical law was re-enacted after the Restoration it never recovered its former influence or power.

As for the many positive proposals of the reformers, they were the only comprehensive attempt to transform the barbaric medieval criminal law before the nineteenth century when many of them were finally adopted by a society in transition to modernity as a consequence of the changes wrought by the Industrial Revolution.

---

8.   *State Tryals. Op. cit.* vol.4. 796.

CHAPTER 6

THE RESTORATION

Significant Changes in the Criminal Law

The Protectorate outlived Oliver Cromwell for less than two years before Charles II came to the throne, amidst great popular excitement in London, in May 1660. The soon-elected Cavalier Parliament moved speedily to accept the principle of the Crown in Parliament which established a new theory of the Constitution. Nothing changed, however, in the concept that effective government meant control of the people by the enforcement of law and order. In the name of the king, Lords Lieutenant at the head of local militia and Justices of the Peace ruled in the counties under the direct supervision of the privy council.

Justices could be appointed only if they were landowners, members of the Church of England and were able to read Latin. One JP sitting alone could imprison all manner of offenders, from vagabonds to persons accused of sedition. The pillory, the whipping post and other local forms of punishment continued to flourish. Two JPs sitting together could inflict more serious punishments and in Quarter Sessions they could fine, imprison and order the transportation of prisoners. Enforcing a large measure of social control they disciplined the country's 10,000 parishes.

Yet the coercion remained fragmented. Remote parts of the country often could not be policed at all. The constables were able to control vagrants but they were powerless against gangs, as was even the militia. The "hue and cry" had largely fallen into disuse. The gentry, with their armed retainers, protected themselves and their property and upheld their power with violence. But much of the criminal law was directed at the poor, and at petty offences which were often considered socially legitimate by large sections of the population. As Daniel Defoe wrote, "the gentry and magistrates of the Kingdom, execute ... laws upon us the poor commons, whilst themselves practising the same crimes, in defiance of the laws both of God and Man, go unpunished."[1]

A case which revealed both continuing religious intolerance and the subjection of juries was that of Benjamin Keach in 1664. He was charged with blasphemy in writing a book for children in which he boldly argued that laymen might preach the gospel and that men and women who could confess their faith might be baptized but not children. The jury were not happy about the prosecution case until the Judge threatened them, whereupon they reached the verdict the Judge required. Keach was then fined £20, imprisoned for two weeks and placed in the pillory twice.[2]

The parliamentary opposition against the use of illegal imprisonment by the earlier prerogative courts had relied upon *Magna Carta* in principle, and the writ of habeas corpus in practice, to show that such arrests were unlawful. Now, however, they were at first generally unsuccessful in the face of the power of the Crown. But during the reign of Charles II the Commons continued to

---

1.   *The Poor Man's Plea.* 7-8.
2.   *State Tryals. Op. cit.* 1017.

assert their rights against the king as declared in Coke's *Petition of Right*. The council, for its part, continued its policy of refusing to accept that the courts could require it to deliver up its prisoners by means of writs of habeas corpus.

Political battle was joined on this issue and the Privy Council began to send its prisoners to remote islands and garrisons to be outside the reach of the courts. This in turn led to the Commons producing a Bill in 1679 which, apparently passed in the Lords only as a result of a miscount, became the famous Habeas Corpus Act.[3] This made statutory the common-law right of a prisoner to be produced before the courts, adding that this must be done within three days, and further providing that no one was to be imprisoned in a place where the writ could not easily be served.

Another important advance had come with *Bushell's Case* in 1670. Jurymen still had to be owners of freehold land to the value of £20 or more. And they were still selected by royal officials. Despite this already considerable control over them by the Crown, jurors remained liable to direct judicial coercion since they could be fined and imprisoned if they refused to convict when directed to do so by the Judge.

Then, in 1670, two Quakers, Penn and Mead, were charged at the Old Bailey with unlawful assembly after Penn had preached a sermon in Gracechurch Street in the City of London. The jury, of whom Edward Bushell was the foreman, would not convict the two men whereupon the Judge had them locked up without food or drink until they changed their minds. When they declined to do so and proceeded to bring in a verdict of not guilty, the Judge fined all 12 of them and had them imprisoned in Newgate gaol.

---

3.   Car.2. c.2.

Bushell and the others responded with a writ of habeas corpus. This came before Lord Justice Vaughan who released them from custody and declared that the verdict of a jury on questions of fact was unassailable, as it remains to this day. If the Judge decides the facts, said Vaughan with unassailable logic, the jury might as well be abolished. "A strange newfound conclusion," he added, "after a [form of] trial so celebrated for many hundreds of years."[4]

With regard to treason, Hale was instrumental in securing some improvement in a vital area. He accepted that an assembly to levy war against the king was treason. But by construction the courts had held that whilst assembling to destroy a particular enclosure was only a riot, to do so for the purpose of casting in all enclosures was levying war against the king.

Hale refused to accept the justice of this and stood out against 10 of his brother Judges in *Messenger's Case*[5] in 1668. For him the riot in this case was only the high-spirited action of an unruly group of eight London apprentices among whom a custom of attempting to pull down a bawdy house or two had long existed. The majority of the Judges prevailed, however, the youths were executed and for a time the law of treason remained dismally elastic. Hale's stand was vindicated seven years later when the Judges accepted that a riot by several hundred weavers in London who had gone about destroying engine looms which they claimed were taking away their jobs was indeed a riot and not treason.

Despite these valuable landmarks in the criminal law, trials continued to be stigmatized by injustice, cruelty and the brutality of Judges. Prisoners were generally assumed to be guilty before and during their trial and in the winter

---

4.   Vaughan's Rep. (1670). 135.
5.   Kelyng. *P.C.* i. 134-5.

of 1683 alone 1,300 Quakers were imprisoned. In *Bushell's Case* the original Judge had said he would like to pull out the foreman's tongue and had praised the Spanish Inquisition. Judges were again dependent on the Crown for their tenure of office, although this had been changed to office "during good behaviour" in the Commonwealth. Perhaps before the Settlement of the Glorious Revolution it made little difference. In any event, cases of political libel proliferated and Chief Justice Scroggs declared that liberty of the press did not exist.

The Popish Plot

A sign of the times was the rapidity with which an alleged Jesuit plot to kill the king and overthrow the government took hold in all sections of the population. In fact the plot was manufactured by Titus Oates, a depraved cleric who had already been found guilty of indecency and perjury, and had himself been plotting with Jesuits in Spain. When he met Charles II, in the course of his trumped-up witch hunt, the king by adroit questioning exposed him as a liar.

Unfortunately, the council proved to be more susceptible, particularly when a reputable, Protestant, London magistrate, Sir Edmondbury Godfrey, was found dead in a field with his sword through his heart after taking depositions from Oates. It was claimed he was killed by Jesuits to stifle the plot. Yet, as a copy of the depositions had been forwarded to the privy council and they were public knowledge, their destruction could not have been the cause of the murder which was never solved.

Charles remained calm under the onslaught but his enemies in Parliament took their cue from Oates and widespread judicial murder and mayhem resulted.

Leading members of the government were either impeached, executed or sent to the Tower, whilst the House of Commons, as if blind to what was happening, continued to express its complete confidence in Oates. Few of those accused of complicity in the plot received a fair trial at the hands of the Judges.

In 1680 Chief Justice Scroggs himself was charged with the "crime" of acquitting four of those who had been accused of treason. In *Articles of High Misdemeanours* which Oates submitted to the council he complained, perhaps with some justice, that Scroggs had browbeaten and curbed him as well as misrepresenting his evidence to the jury so that they found the prisoners not guilty against the evidence. No action was taken by the council but the Articles were used as a basis for proceedings in the House of Commons where Scroggs was impeached.[6] However, Parliament was prorogued with the result that he merely lost his office and not his head.

Six years later a Samuel Johnson (not related to *the* Dr. Johnson) was brought before the King's Bench for publishing two seditious libels. He had written a "Humble Address to English Protestants in the Army" claiming that they were under the command of French and Irish papists. He suffered a £500 fine and was sent to prison until he paid it, which the Judges knew he was unable to do. He was also placed in the pillory and whipped from Newgate to Tyburn with nine cords made into 317 knots.[7] On June 11, 1689 the Convention Parliament revoked the judgment as being cruel and illegal and released him from prison. The new king promptly gave him £1,000 in compensation together with £300 a year out of the Post Office for his and his son's lives.

The tragedy of the Popish Plot was that the country

---

6.   *State Tryals. Op. cit.* vol.7. 479.
7.   *Ibid.* 645.

had become seized in a panic for bloody revenge against a host of innocent "plotters" conjured up in the fevered imaginations of the only true plotters, Oates and his confederates. Eventually the alarm subsided and Oates, who was fortunate that no capital charge was brought against him, was tried in two cases for perjury when the juries had no difficulty in finding him guilty.

After the second trial before four Judges, including Judge Jeffreys, he was fined heavily, sent to the pillory, whipped from Aldgate to Newgate and, two days later, from Newgate to Tyburn. In all he received over 2,000 lashes and was then imprisoned for life. It was a severe sentence but he suffered less than the many whom he sent to the gallows by his mendacity and he received scant sympathy from those who had so recently applauded him. He was, however, released from prison in 1688 and after pleading for a pension was, incredibly, given one, albeit only £5.

Also in this post-Commonwealth period there appeared the only serious blot on the career of Sir Matthew Hale. In 1665 two widows, Rose Callender and Amy Duny, came for trial before the Chief Baron at the Bury St Edmunds Assizes on charges of witchcraft. Seven children, who were too young to give evidence themselves, were said by the prosecution to have been bewitched by the accused. It was claimed, for example, that a witch in the shape of a bee had flown on to the face of one of the children who thereupon "vomited up a twopenny nail with a very broad head."

Another child was said to have vomited up at least 30 pins on one occasion. Even more startling to be accepted as evidence was the allegation that a child had thrown an invisible mouse into a fire where it had exploded. An invisible duck was also caught and burnt. Although it was established in court that all the allegations were fraudulent and that there was no true evidence against the widows they were found guilty by the jury and executed - still protesting their innocence. Significantly, within half an hour of the verdicts all the children had recovered from their ailments.

All that can be said in mitigation for Hale in declining to throw out the case is that hundreds of alleged witches were executed in that century, and Matthew Hopkins, witch-hunter extraordinary, had been particularly active in Suffolk and Essex in fabricating evidence against them, and extracting it by torture. Sixty were hanged in one year alone, including an Anglican clergyman aged 80.

Hale was in no doubt that witches existed and deserved their fate since ch.22 of the *Book of Exodus* said, "Thou shalt not suffer a witch to live." It remains a sad lapse for Hale who must have had some qualms about the evidence against the women since he declined to review it for the jury. The reaction against numerous trials such as this was so strong that in 1736 the laws against witchcraft were repealed. It is interesting to note that executioners were widely considered in Europe to be immune from the spells of witches since burning them produced no ill effects. Indeed, it was thought that when a person was condemned to death the executioner's sword would rattle in its longing for blood. The blood of a victim of the gallows was said to cure epilepsy and many a hangman was asked to perform medical treatment.[8]

The Game Laws were a clear illustration of the class nature of the criminal law. Game laws had existed from the fourteenth century when the Game Act of 1389 was passed. The Game Act of 1671 was to preserve this harsh law until the middle of the nineteenth century. By this latter Act, it was made illegal for anyone other than a wealthy landowner and his heirs to take game. Poaching was, of course, widespread but the real iniquity of the Act

8.   *Cf.* P. Spierenburg. *The Spectacle of Suffering.* 30. 1984.

was that the country gentry and aristocrats who owned the land were also both Judge and jury when sitting as JPs trying those brought before them.

In 1828 Brougham was moved to say:

> There is not a worse-constituted tribunal on the face of the earth, not even that of the Turkish Cadi, than that at which summary convictions on the Game Laws constantly take place; I mean a bench or a brace of sporting justices. I am far from saying that, on such subjects, they are activated by corrupt motives; but they are undoubtedly instigated by their abhorrence of the poacher. From their decisions on those points, where their passions are most likely to mislead them, no appeal in reality lies to a more calm and unprejudiced tribunal.[9]

The sentences of the justices were frequently savage in their own interests and a starving man with a starving family could find himself either fined and imprisoned or transported, in each case with his family left destitute. The hunt for game was more important to these custodians of the law than human beings. Blackstone, who was no critic of the law, felt sufficiently incensed to write of poaching as, "an offence which the sportsmen of England seem to think of the highest importance; and a matter, perhaps the only one, of general and national concern."[10]

Judge Jeffreys

With the reign of James II we come to the most infamous

---

9.   *Speeches.* ii. 373.

10.   *Comm. Op. cit.* iv. 174.

of the trials and punishments of the late seventeenth century, the "Bloody Assize" of the Western Circuit. Ironically, on his accession James had announced his intention of preserving all the just rights and liberties of the nation. It is only just, therefore, in deploring the excesses and ferocity of Lord Chief Justice Jeffreys in the "Bloody Assize", to remember that at all times he was carrying out the instructions of the king, albeit with his own brand of enthusiasm and vigour.

The ill-fated rebellion of the Duke of Monmouth was suppressed easily and speedily. He landed with a small force at Lyme Regis on June 11, 1685, collected a number of West Country supporters, and was defeated at Sedgemore on July 6. The first hint of the blood that was to follow in the sequel came with the trial of 70-year-old Dame Alice Lisle, the widow of Judge Lisle, at the Great Hall in Winchester Castle on August 27. Here she was accused of concealing a rebel, at her home at Moyle Court in Hampshire, before he had even been charged, let alone found guilty.

At the trial before the dreaded Chief Justice, Jeffreys himself took over from the prosecution and proceeded with a ruthless cross-examination of the frail widow. At one point when a witness in her defence was giving evidence Jeffreys barked, "Hold up the lantern, that we may see his brazen face." Despite all his intimidation, however, at the conclusion of the trial the jury were reluctant to convict and were forced to retire three times before they could be persuaded to return a verdict of guilty after a doubtful ruling of law by the Judge. The following morning Jeffreys sentenced Lady Lisle to be burned to death that afternoon. She immediately wrote to the king for mercy but she was beheaded on September 2, the change from being burned to losing her head being the maximum mercy the king could summon up.

Two days later the Lord Chief Justice entered

Dorchester. As some 2,600 prisoners were awaiting trial there and at other Assize towns, the Judge, who was anxious to return to London and advance his career on the impending death of Guilford, the Lord Chancellor, let it be known that if they pleaded not guilty but were convicted they would suffer the death penalty, whereas if they pleaded guilty they would be transported. Sixty-eight thereupon pleaded guilty and were duly sent to the West Indies as slaves. Thirty pleaded not guilty and were hanged on September 7. Only one was acquitted. Jeffreys' conduct in court was ferocious and he boasted that he had got through 98 trials in the one day.

The terror was now unmistakable and more and more prisoners pleaded guilty. On September 10, the last day of the Dorchester Assize, 238 were brought before Jeffreys for sentence. Sixty-one of these were mercilessly hanged, drawn and quartered publicly at the chief towns of the county and the remainder transported.

Taunton, which was Jeffreys' next important port of call, was frozen with horror. Only a few were hardy enough to defy their tormentor and declare their innocence in spite of his threats. Of the more than 500 who pleaded guilty, 139 were sentenced to immediate death despite his earlier promise. The remainder were transported to the financial benefit of members of the king's court who received substantial payments for each of these prisoners whom they sold to contractors for shipment to the West Indies as colonial slaves.

Jeffreys himself was paid £1,416 for his ghoulish labours and accepted an enormous bribe of £15,000 for securing a pardon for Edmund Prideaux, a wealthy West Country Whig landowner. Part of this sum the Lord Chief Justice used in the purchase of estates in Leicestershire which were called by some *Alcedama*, after the Biblical field of blood.

Throughout the "Bloody Assize" 1,381 men were

convicted of treason, of whom 350 were barbarously executed and over 800 sold into slavery. None of this prevented Jeffreys from being elevated to the Woolsack to become Lord Chancellor, indeed it eased his progress. Nemesis followed, however, in December 1688 when, as Chancellor, he attempted to emulate James in fleeing abroad to escape from the new Revolution. He was recognized and seized on the Thames at Wapping and incarcerated in the Tower where he died and was buried at the age of 41.

CHAPTER 7

GLORIOUS REVOLUTION TO REPRESSION

Changing Attitudes to Punishment

To avoid the Catholic succession to the throne plotted by James, leaders of both the Whigs and the Tories invited William, Prince of Orange, to replace the king and to enforce both the law and the Protestant religion in England. Already prepared, William landed at the small fishing port of Brixham in Devon in 1688 and brought to pass a revolution without a single shot being fired. A Convention was then called in London which offered the throne to William and Mary in February 1689. This was accompanied in both the Commons and the Lords by a Declaration of Rights which was later embodied in the Bill of Rights which ranks second only to *Magna Carta* as a charter of liberty and on occasion is still referred to in the judgments of our courts.

The Declaration forbade a standing army in peacetime without the consent of Parliament. It provided for the free election of MPs and their complete freedom of speech in the House of Commons which it settled was to meet frequently; and for jurors to be empanelled fairly. By cl.10 it further provided, "that excessive bail ought not to be required, nor excessive fines imposed; nor cruel and unusual punishments inflicted." Then, in 1701, the Act of Settlement completed the process by establishing the independence of the judiciary.

This peaceful "Glorious Revolution" signalled the partial triumph of the disciplined power of the propertied Whigs over royal despotism and the nobility. At last the common law was to be supreme over the prerogative and the rule of law began to displace royal discrimination. Although the king was to retain important powers, including the appointment of Ministers, henceforth he was a constitutional monarch subject to the law, as Bracton and Coke had long ago maintained he was.

Despite these fundamental changes, however, the criminal law remained an instrument of the state to be used to ensure the acquiescence of the people in the new alignment in class relations and power. For instance, during the trial of Dr. Sacheverell for preaching a violent High Church sermon in 1709, a crowd assembled outside his lodging in the Temple and moved on to burn down the meeting-house of a Protestant dissenting minister. Demaree, one of the leaders of the crowd, was found guilty of treason as a consequence. So too was a man named Purchase who had come on the scene rather late, and drunk. Finding such conduct to be high treason (despite Hale's earlier success to the contrary) was no aberration by the courts since it was confirmed by Lord Mansfield in the trial of Lord George Gordon following the anti-Catholic Gordon Riots in 1780.

Nevertheless, there were subtle changes occurring in public attitudes and some improvements in criminal procedure followed. For the first time an accused person was allowed to decline to answer questions and was permitted to cross-examine witnesses as well as call sworn witnesses in his own defence. Furthermore, hearsay evidence was coming to be distrusted and jurors, who were now more often drawn from the very wealthy groups of society, had entirely ceased to be witnesses and were expected to judge the evidence. By judicial pronouncements, Sir John Holt, who became Chief Justice of the King's Bench although he declined William's offer to appoint him Lord Chancellor, encouraged this process. He established the rule that evidence of previous convictions against an accused person should not be admitted before the verdict, and also held that prisoners should no longer be kept in irons during their trial.

He invited prisoners in the dock to interrupt him if they thought he was not stating their case fairly to the jury. And, in a significant decision in the case of *Smith v. Browne*[1] he declared that, "as soon as a Negro comes into England, he is free" even if he came in as a slave. It is noteworthy also that he always secured an acquittal in the trials of witches he presided over. In a remarkable tribute to Holt for the time Richard Steele wrote in the *Tatler*, "the prisoner knew ... that his Judge would wrest no law to destroy him, nor conceal any that could save him."[2] The cruelty of earlier Judges whose tenure of office had been dependent on pleasing the king had been moderated.

The Whig Supremacy

Nonetheless, under the Hanovers the criminal law continued to be illogical and brutal whilst the function of government, according to the accepted philosophy of John Locke, was the "preservation of property."[3] Dr. W.A. Speck has shown that, "England's governors came from a very narrow social stratum. The levers of power were

---

1.   Holt K.B. 495.
2.   No.14. May 12, 1709.
3.   *An Essay concerning the True, Original, Extent and End of Civil Government*. 239. 1689.

in the hands of a few hundred families who between them controlled the machinery of government."[4] They were part of the landed aristocracy, whose leaders Disraeli called the "Venetian oligarchy", in whose hands both George I and George II were mere puppets.

Few statutes were enacted in this period but an Act of 1716 made it a capital offence to mutilate trees which ornamented gentlemen's gardens. Another, in 1720, made combinations of journeymen tailors for raising wages or reducing hours illegal on pain of imprisonment. Wages were fixed by the Act[5] at between one shilling and eightpence and two shillings a day. Hours of work were set from 6 a.m. to 8 p.m. with an hour for lunch. Similar statutes were passed to regulate the wages and conditions of hat makers, silk weavers and others. JPs continued to act as local despots and one, sitting alone, could, without a trial, have vagrants whipped, fined and committed to the stocks for swearing, drunkenness or falling foul of the Game Laws.

The ubiquitous pillory remained in constant use, including for the offence of a husband selling his wife, and still remained unequal in its effect as a punishment. For instance, whilst in 1732 a man was killed in the pillory by spectators at Seven Dials in London (a by no means uncommon occurrence), by contrast in 1758 a Dr. Shebbeare stood in the pillory attended by a servant in livery who held an umbrella over his head to protect him from nothing more menacing than the rain.

Only with the arrival of modern commerce did death become the punishment for a first offence of forgery. Hence earlier, in 1731, Sir Peter Stranger stood in the pillory at Charing Cross for forging a deed. After an hour he was taken to the scaffold where the hangman used a

---

4.   *Stability and Strife. England 1714-1760.* 143. 1977.
5.   7 Geo.I. st.1. c.13.

pruning knife to cut off both his ears, and a pair of
scissors to slit both his nostrils. All of this he bore with
great patience but when his right nostril was seared with
a hot iron the pain was so violent he could not bear it and
his left nostril was left untouched.

He was then carried bleeding to a nearby tavern where,
after his wound had been dressed by a surgeon, he was
"as merry at dinner with his friends as if nothing had
happened."[6] The notorious and celebrated Dr. William
Dodd, on the other hand, was executed in June 1777 for
forging a bond, despite a widespread public outcry and
a moving intervention by Dr. Samuel Johnson.

The death penalty remained the punishment for all
felonies when Prime Minister Sir Robert Walpole,
despised for his unprincipled exercise of power and sheer
greed, secured the passing of the Waltham Black Act in
1723.[7] This hideous statute added some 50 new capital
offences to the criminal law to make a total of over 200
for which death was the penalty. Thus was born what
became known as the penal law's "bloody code". The
offences the statute was directed at were already
adequately covered by the existing law and included going
armed and disguised (merely a handkerchief over the
mouth was sufficient) on the highway or on open common
ground, or in forests, parks and enclosed grounds, to kill
or steal deer, or break down the head of any fishpond.[8]

In essentials it was simply an Act to provoke terror.
It was used against persons who were not disguised and
who were not criminals. Most of those convicted under its
provisions were men of respectable occupations and only
one of those brought to trial had a previous criminal

---

6.   Andrew Amos. *Op. cit.* 221.
7.   9 Geo.I. c.22.
8.   For Walpole's personal interest in the Act to preserve his hunting
        rights, *cf.* E.P. Thompson, *Whigs and Hunters*. 1975.

record. It was a blatant example of class control and discipline and, although it was enacted in the interests of a small property-hungry group of *nouveau riche* individuals around Walpole, it was not found desirable to repeal it until 1823.

The Murder Act of 1752 gave Judges a discretion to have a murderer executed and have his corpse hung publicly in a gibbet all within 48 hours of the sentence. In another attempt at terror it also required the bodies of those executed murderers who were not gibbeted to be delivered to the surgeons for dissection - a fate which caused dread amongst the ordinary people who were immersed in the superstitions and mystique of death and the integrity of the corpse.

John Wilkes

When George III ascended the throne in 1760 he set about attempting to retrieve the royal power which he believed had been so carelessly allowed to lapse by his two predecessors. George Grenville accepted office as Prime Minister precisely in order to help free the king from the restraints of the powerful oligarchies previously in control of government. The Opposition, however, received advance notice of the Ministry's new policy as set out in the King's Speech and to combat it with the maximum of publicity sought the help of John Wilkes. Wilkes was editor of the malevolent *North Briton* and, prompted by the elder Pitt, published his famous issue No. 45 of that journal on April 23, 1763. In this he branded the speech as falsehood. Wilkes became to George III what Becket had been to Henry II.

Grenville chose to treat Wilkes' article as a personal attack on the king and secured a General Warrant for the arrest of Wilkes and his printers. Such a warrant did not name the persons to be arrested or even their offence, in this case the publication of No. 45. True to its name the warrant permitted arrests indiscriminately. On the seizure of Wilkes, his friends obtained a writ of habeas corpus but the government concealed him in the Tower in an attempt to evade it. The trick did not succeed for long, however, and on obtaining his freedom, Wilkes claimed to be immune from arrest as a Member of Parliament since he had not committed treason, felony or breach of the peace.

When he was brought before Sir John Pratt, the Chief Justice of the Common Pleas, he was released on that basis. In a reserved judgment the Chief Justice later proceeded to rule that general warrants were illegal, as they have remained ever since. Wilkes, who obtained substantial damages for false imprisonment, had scored a signal constitutional victory. Nonetheless, in November, after he had republished No. 45, the House of Commons voted that the publication was a seditious libel. They ordered that it be burnt by the public hangman in front of the Royal Exchange where he and the Sheriff of London suffered gross indignities at the hands of the populace who prevented the burning from taking place.

The following year Wilkes was tried for seditious and obscene libels (the latter for his *Essay on Woman)* in the King's Bench. The trial had to take place in his absence since he was ill in France and he was found guilty and outlawed - a punishment still in use after more than a thousand years. Subsequently Wilkes went on to other parliamentary battles that are not relevant here. He also worked with the *Society of Supporters of the Bill of Rights,* and helped to secure both the freedom to publish parliamentary debates and the birth of the new reforming Whig Party. We may observe that Gladstone was to say that whether we liked it or not the name of Wilkes was enrolled amongst the greatest champions of English freedom.

In a passing note on the punishments of the time, it may be observed that the Old Bailey proceedings of December 1762 to October 1763 record trials of 433 persons for the crimes of murder, robbery and theft. Of these 243 were convicted with 42 men and five women sentenced to death, 122 men and 49 women to be transported, 10 men and two women branded and five women whipped.

Prisons

Common gaols at this time, with a few exceptions, were still the responsibility of the local authorities and the justices whose chief concern was to see that they did not become a burden on the rates. They were not intended for punishment as such but principally for holding persons securely on remand pending trial and for those who could not pay their fines or debts. In the main they were disreputable places of squalor, filth and privation. There were some 200 in the country and they were to be found in dungeons, cellars of municipal and market buildings, cages, inns and gatehouses. All were in the control of private gaolers.

According to Lionel W. Fox[9] the only duty of the gaoler to the prisoners was to hold them and his only interest to make what he could from them. Gaolers took a fee on the admission of prisoners and, if they were fortunate enough to leave as free men, another on their discharge. It was a common sight to see acquitted prisoners dragged back to their cells until they could pay their release fees. Chaining in irons in gaol was a frequent practice and gaolers took a further fee for hammering the irons on and

---

9.　　*The English Prison and Borstal Systems.* 21. 1952.

another for knocking them off.

A price had to be paid for food and improved accommodation, and alcohol, tobacco and women were in plentiful supply for those able and willing to pay.[10] Such prisons were houses of lechery, debauchery, moral corruption, and the contagious pestilence of typhus known as "gaol fever" brought about by absence of sanitation, bad diet, vermin, and lack of fresh air and washing facilities. We know that at the "black sessions" of the Old Bailey in 1750 four of the six Judges, three counsel, an under-sheriff, several jurors and a number of spectators all died of typhus contracted in court. And it was computed that every year a quarter of all prisoners were thus destroyed.[11] In 1773-74 more died from gaol fever than were executed. "Thus perish yearly," wrote the *Gentleman's Magazine* in January 1759, "five thousand men, overborne with sorrow, consumed by famine or putrefied by filth."

It was into this picture that John Howard stepped when, as High Sheriff of Bedfordshire, he began to examine the prisons in his county. Michael Ignatieff has painted a grim portrait of Howard's personality in his fine book *A Just Measure of Pain* (1989). But his influence for good was considerable. The scenes which greeted him in the county gaols appalled him and impelled him into travelling to inspect prisons throughout the country and in parts of Europe in order to expose the evils he depicted and propose remedies. In 1777 he published what he had witnessed together with his conclusions in *The State of the Prisons in England and Wales with some Preliminary Observations, and an Account of some Foreign Prisons.*

---

10.   For an account of debauchery at Newgate *cf.* "Finding Solace in Eighteenth Century Newgate" W.J. Sheehan in *Crime in England 1550-1800.* ed. J.S. Cockburn 229-45. 1977.

11.   Fox *Op. cit.* 21.

Howard proposed that gaolers should be paid a regular salary instead of being obliged to extract fees and that prisoners should be segregated at night but allowed association during the day. They should be permitted to do useful work in proper workshops and be given adequate food. But enforcement was to remain in the hands of the justices. The overriding aim was to combine discipline with humanity. The justices, however, still feared for the rates and at this stage no effective reforms were introduced.

Nevertheless, *The State of the Prisons* made a lasting impression on middle-class and humanitarian thought. When Howard, who was a non-conformist landowner with a developed social conscience, died in the Ukraine after inspecting hospital conditions there Jeremy Bentham said of him that, "he died a martyr after living an apostle." Some of Howard's proposals were indeed incorporated in statutes encouraged by William Eden, later Lord Aukland, but they were permissive not mandatory and remained more inspirational than effective.

Beccaria's Crusade

Whilst imprisonment was not yet seen as an alternative punishment to the death penalty the whole question of the bleak inhumanity of the penal law was raised to startling effect by Count Cesare Beccaria, a 26-year-old Italian nobleman with no legal experience, with his book *Dei Delitte e delle Pene* ("Of Crimes and Punishments"), written in 1764. Published anonymously at first for fear of serious reprisals, the book was a brilliant indictment from which the crusade against capital punishment was to take flight. Not surprisingly the Inquisition forbade its publication under pain of death and called Beccaria a madman and a stupid impostor. The work was stigmatized as having, "sprung from the deepest abyss of darkness, horrible, monstrous, full of poison."

The Church argued that torture was a mercy to the criminal since it purged him in his death from the sin of falsehood. In most of Europe proof of guilt was sought almost exclusively from secret accusations and torments both ingenious and gruesome. Beccaria exposed torture to ridicule and asked how the truth could reside, "... in the muscles and fibres of a wretch in torture. By this method," he continued, "the robust will escape, and the feeble be condemned. These are the inconveniences of this pretended test of truth worthy only of a cannibal."[12] Despite the strictures of the Church, Beccaria was to savour success when torture was abolished in Lombardy, Austria, Portugal, Sweden, Russia and France as a direct result of his inspiration. In all these countries his work destroyed the prevailing system.

To Beccaria punishments were necessary both to prevent society plunging into chaos and to defend public liberty. But, equally, any punishment which was not absolutely necessary was tyrannical. The end of punishment, he said, was solely to prevent the criminal doing further injury to society and to prevent others committing similar offences. Such punishment should make a lasting impression on the minds of others with the least torment to the body of the criminal.

And as the only reasonable basis for punishment was its effectiveness as a deterrent the death penalty was useless. It was itself a barbarous act of violence and an injustice since it rendered an act legitimate in payment for an equivalent act of violence. "Countries and times most notorious for the severity of punishments," he continued, "were always those in which the most bloody and inhuman actions and the most atrocious crimes were

---

12.   *Of Crimes and Punishments.* 58. 1769 edn.

committed; for the hand of the legislator and that of the assassin were directed by the same spirit of ferocity."[13]

To avoid being an act of violence, he concluded, every punishment, "... should be public, immediate and necessary; the least possible in the case; proportioned to the crime, and determined by the laws."[14] Its primary purpose was to benefit society, not to torment offenders.

Not only were secret trials and torture the rule on the Continent before Beccaria's onslaught, but evidence was often flimsy and the Judges had unlimited discretion as to punishment. In this context Beccaria's proposals were both humane and revolutionary as the Church immediately recognized. Their impact spread like wildfire throughout Europe where more liberal penal codes were speedily enacted.

Not in England, however, where the defence of property was still the principal purpose of punishment. Blackstone merely mentioned Beccaria in passing and thought that punishment should be increased where temptation was greater. Thus theft of a handkerchief from the person should result in death whilst theft of a more valuable load of hay merited transportation.[15] And, in 1775, Archdeacon Paley unfurled the ideological colours of a criminal-law system actually centred on capital punishment.[16]

Justice, said this Doctor of Divinity, must be left to God. To prevent crimes man's laws should provide capital punishment for every crime which, under any circumstances, might merit death. The Judges should act with discrimination in sentencing but by means of this threat hanging over the crimes of many, "the tenderness

---

13.   *Ibid.* 99.
14.   *Ibid.* 179.
15.   *Comm.* iv.
16.   *Principles of Moral and Political Philosophy.* vi. c.9. 526. 2nd edn. 1786.

of the law cannot be taken advantage of." Paley described his design for a multiplicity of capital offences as being based on "wisdom and humanity." And, as an example of such humanity, he went on to advocate that murderers should meet death by being thrown into a den of wild beasts where they would perish in a manner dreadful to the imagination but concealed from view!

One may well wonder what kind of world Paley was living in, yet his advocacy was to have a profound influence in England for nearly a century. His book was dedicated to the Bishop of Carlisle, the father of Lord Ellenborough whose speeches in the House of Lords both defended and followed Paley's doctrine. When Samuel Romilly endeavoured to refute Paley's philosophy in the House of Commons William Windham MP responded that it "had done more for the moral improvement of mankind than perhaps the writings of any other man that had ever existed.[17] According to T.R. Birks, Paley's book "reigned widely in England for nearly half a century as the best modern work on ethical science."[18] It was adopted as a textbook by Cambridge University, and it ran through 15 editions in Paley's own lifetime.

In fact, the philosophy of Paley was welcome to the ruling aristocracy who, with their immense holdings in land and long memories of the Stuarts and Cromwell, would not tolerate the idea of a regular police force to deter people from crime. They continued instead to rely upon the abundance of discretionary capital laws to protect their interests. The middle class, on the other hand, sought to promote the philosophical movement for the reduction of, and certainty in, all punishments which Beccaria had inspired. As we shall see the issue was only finally resolved in the nineteenth century.

---

17.   *Hansard.* vol.15. col.371.
18.   *Modern Utilitarianism.* 48. 1874.

The Rights of Man

Towards the end of the eighteenth century the thoughts of some leading statesmen, including Pitt the Younger, were turning towards reform. This was not surprising after nearly a century of rule by oligarchies and now with a king who dreamed of a return to rule by divine right. When the French Revolution broke out it was widely believed in England that France might be following the example of the Glorious Revolution and would arrive at a constitutional monarchy. Then the turn of events seemed to suggest a prospect more akin to 1649 and regicide.

If the former occurred, would it inflame the common people and win support from the middle class of England, both of whom had sympathized openly with the colonists in the American War of Independence? Edmund Burke sounded the alarm with his *Reflections on the French Revolution*, published in 1790, and his rejection of the rights of the "swinish multitude."

Thomas Paine responded. Born at Thetford in Norfolk in 1737 he had emigrated to America where his pamphlet *Common Sense* had stiffened the resolve of George Washington's army at a crucial moment in the war and led to Paine making the first draft of the Declaration of Independence. Having returned to England by 1790 Paine wrote a rejoinder to Burke entitled *The Rights of Man* in 1792.

Burke had argued that the Settlement of 1689 had established the form of the English Constitution "for ever". Paine retorted that the legislators might as well have passed an Act to enable themselves to live for ever. It seems incredible but over a million and a half copies of Paine's book sold like hot cakes. This galvanized the government into action. The militias were mobilized, justices were told to seek out all distributors of seditious writings and the Attorney-General instituted proceedings against Paine for seditious libel.

This was meant to be preliminary to a charge of high treason and Paine's friend, the poet William Blake, convinced him that he was as good as dead if he did not go at once to Paris where he had been elected to the National Convention. Paine removed himself to France accordingly and in his absence the trial commenced on December 18, 1792, when he was represented by the formidable Thomas Erskine. To say that the people did not already have all the rights they needed, said the Attorney-General, was in effect levying war upon the Crown and the Constitution. On the contrary, replied Erskine, Fox's Libel Act of 1792 showed that a published work genuinely written to benefit mankind could not ever be a libel.

The special jury had been selected by the Crown lawyers and they found Paine guilty before the Judge had even had an opportunity to sum up the case! Prosecutions were now launched against printers, publishers and booksellers throughout the land. A barrister named John Frost was disbarred, placed in the pillory and imprisoned for six months for saying, in echoes of John Lilburne, that equality was every Englishman's birthright and he was for equality and no king.

Thus did the interest in political reform of Pitt the Younger and his government come to an abrupt end. Instead retrenchment and repression became the order of the day. At this stage the Enlightenment had made little impact on England and the aristocracy, anxious about the turn of events in France, kept a tight grip on society for the next two or three decades.

Trials of Radicals

The law of treason, even in these more modern times,

continued to be used as a means of social and political control. Two years later Thomas Hardy, Secretary of the Radical London Corresponding Society, was brought to trial on a charge of high treason. As part of the psychological warfare against Hardy, Pitt took to the House of Commons three huge sealed bags of captured documents and a message from the king requiring the enactment of a Special Powers Act. Yet Hardy had merely called a Convention to advocate universal suffrage and annual Parliaments and had said nothing against the king.

His trial for "compassing the king's death" commenced at the Old Bailey on October 25, 1794. Erskine was again the defence lawyer and, among others, the Duke of Richmond and Richard Sheridan gave evidence that they supported the aims of the Convention and spoke of the law-abiding character of Hardy. This time the jury had no difficulty in finding for the prisoner. Foolishly the government now decided to proceed against Horne Tooke who was a co-accused of Hardy. He produced the same witnesses and also the Bishop of Gloucester, Earl Stanhope, Earl Camden and Charles James Fox.

Tooke had a reputation as a joker and a wit and he must have enjoyed the irony and the pleasure of calling a further witness by subpoena, William Pitt himself. Pitt was obliged to admit, reluctantly, that he had once attended a meeting of delegates from all over the country to recommend the calling of a reform Parliament. Not surprisingly Horne Tooke was also acquitted, to the acclaim of the crowds of London. It seems clear that the two juries thought that there was no treason and that the penalty for high treason was out of all proportion to the actual offences alleged, since generally the thinking of juries was now more closely in line with that of the Judges. In any event the government reluctantly scrapped some 800 warrants for arrest which had been prepared for immediate use.

Before long the economic effects of the war with France were taking their toll on the lives of the people on this side of the Channel. Hunger riots broke out, Ireland was in revolt and the fleet mutinied at Spithead. The government responded by suspending habeas corpus, which was not restored for eight years, and in 1799 enacted the Unlawful Societies Act[19] which provided that (apart from Quakers) *every* society which had branches or sections was an unlawful combination. The penalty for membership was three months' imprisonment imposed by summary jurisdiction.

This Act suppressed by name the London Corresponding Society, the United Irishmen and many other societies. It was interpreted by the courts to mean that trade unions also were illegal, but they spared Orange Lodges. James Fitzjames Stephen was later to say that in his day (1882) societies such as the Law Society could be held to be unlawful under the Act. In the meantime the provision it contained against unlawful oaths was used in conjunction with the Mutiny Act of 1797 to secure the conviction and transportation for seven years of the Tolpuddle Martyrs in 1834 for combining to resist a reduction in their wages.

Sir Samuel Romilly

The second half of the eighteenth century also witnessed a strengthening of the penal laws and an extension of the incidence of the death penalty. Times were hard and a rapid impoverishment of the poor was perceived as a cause of the growth in crime. Describing the hunger, cold, nakedness, filth and disease of whole families Henry

---

19.   38 Geo.3. c.79.

Fielding concluded, "they starve, and freeze and rot among themselves; but they beg, and steal and rob among their betters."[20]

Smollett, in his *History of England,* described the land as infested with robbers, assassins and incendiaries, "the natural consequence of degeneracy, corruption and want of police in the interior government of the kingdom."[21] And Sir James Mackintosh was later to write of this period that if he could do nothing else every Member of Parliament could create a capital felony.[22] Indeed, there is a great deal of evidence to show that numerous capital statutes were passed into law at this time without any debate whatsoever.

William Eden, in his *Principles of Penal Law* written in 1771, sought to win support for the ideals of Beccaria by advocating that vindictive justice was shocking. He, in turn, was given support by Samuel Romilly who had a more significant impact. Romilly, a reforming barrister and at one time Solicitor-General, wholeheartedly accepted the principles of Beccaria and spent his life trying to mitigate the severity of the penal laws. Stigmatizing capital punishment as a "lottery of justice", he attacked the demand of the Rev. Martin Madan that all capital laws should be rigidly enforced. Madan's book, *Thoughts on Executive Justice* (1785) had a considerable influence on the Judges which produced a temporary bloodbath. In the year before it was published, 51 persons were executed in London alone whilst in the year following the number had risen to 97.

Romilly, without waiting for the statistics, was stung in reply to publish an essay entitled, *Observations on a*

---

20.   *A Proposal for Making an Effectual Provision for the Poor etc.* 10. 1753.

21.   Vol.iv. 40. 1794.

22.   *Miscellaneous Works.* iii. 371. 1846.

Late Publication (1786) in which he argued for imprisonment instead of death for most felonies. Ahead of most of his contemporaries he thought that excessive severity increased crime rather than deterring it. Only 100 copies of Romilly's reply were sold but he sent a copy to each of the Judges and the number of executions fell back.

"Madan's relentlessness" wrote Romilly, "breathes a spirit contrary to the genius of the present times." His doctrine was not supported by dispassionate argument; instead he used far-fetched hyperboles, ferocious language, and "all the most specious colouring of rhetoric." Romilly also attacked Paley's theories and introduced Bill after Bill in the House of Commons to remove the death penalty for specified offences. All were then again and again destroyed in the House of Lords where the Bishops, Lord Chancellor Eldon and Lord Chief Justice Ellenborough joined forces as followers of Paley to defeat them.

Writing of the opposition of the Archbishop of Canterbury and other named bishops to a Bill to abolish capital punishment for the crime of stealing to the value of five shillings in a shop, Romilly wrote:

> I rank these prelates amongst the members who were solicited to vote against the Bill, because I would rather be convinced of their servility towards government, than that, recollecting the mild doctrines of their religion, they could have come down to the House spontaneously, to vote that transportation for life is not a sufficiently severe punishment for the offence of pilfering what is of five shillings' value, and that nothing but the blood of the offender can afford an adequate atonement for such a transgression.[23]

---

23.   *Memoirs.* ii. 331. 1840.

When Lord Ellenborough opposed a Bill to abolish the pillory, holding up its antiquity as a merit and declaiming against any innovation in the criminal law, Romilly asked whether if he had lived some time before he would have been in favour of such bulwarks of the Constitution as embowelling alive or the burning of women alive, and if the removal of these bulwarks had endangered the Constitution.[24]

He was appalled that Ellenborough, who guided the Judges, had indicated that they were being too lenient in their use of the death penalty. And that he could speak of transportation as a punishment which had few terrors for those who violated the law and, "was only a summer airing by an easy migration to a milder climate."[25]

Romilly made outstanding speeches in the House of Commons for reform of both the substantive criminal law and criminal procedure. He had some successes but largely failed against powerful and entrenched opposition. Nonetheless, he inspired a generation of reformers who ultimately achieved a revolutionary breakthrough in the nineteenth century. And when he committed suicide after the death of his beloved wife his work was taken up by Mackintosh, Fowell Buxton and the Whig legal reformer Dr. Stephen Lushington. His memory is undimmed and he endures as a renowned figure in the history of penal law reform.

---

24.   *Speeches*. i. 472. 1820.
25.   *Memoirs. Op.cit.* 333-4.

CHAPTER 8

TOWARDS A MODERN SOCIETY

Inspiration of Jeremy Bentham

Although a great deal has been written here about changes in the criminal and penal laws over the centuries, they had largely remained cruel and disordered. There was no real achievement to record. With the coming of the nineteenth century, however, a shift could be discerned. The Enlightenment had altered men's opinions and values and imperceptibly the industrial revolution was changing their social, economic and political lives.

With law, the extraordinary catalyst of change was Jeremy Bentham. Born on February 15, 1748, in Red Lion Street, Houndsditch in East London, Bentham had a feeble, dwarfish body but a dazzling mind. An infant prodigy, at the age of three he was found seated at a desk reading Rapin's huge folio *History of England* with a lighted candle on each side of him. He was at Lincoln's Inn by the age of 16 having been the youngest graduate until then at Oxford. But, in opposition to Blackstone and his contentment with "this noble pile", as he called the Constitution,[1] Bentham came to despise the unwritten

---

1. *Op. cit.* end.

common law with its judicial law-making. He decided to set out to replace it with a science of law based on logic and clarity of expression, seasoned with humanity.

With his utilitarian philosophy of the greatest happiness of the greatest number, he encouraged Romilly, Brougham and Peel in law reform and, starting from first principles, turned his own inventive mind to the task of codifying the rules of government and law in their entirety. We shall meet some of his proposals as we proceed and we can safely accept the verdict of Brougham that "the age of law reform and the age of Jeremy Bentham are one and the same."[2] His was a seminal influence in a time which saw the birth of modern industry, the American War of Independence, the French Revolution, *The Wealth of Nations,* the influence of the Enlightenment, and the Reform Act of 1832.

The early years of the nineteenth century revealed little improvement in the criminal law and its penalties. The ruling aristocracy, with the impact of the French Revolution still fresh in their minds, were fearful of the serious rioting and unrest which economic distress was causing, as well as the potential power of the growing working class.

The Luddite Riots, which commenced in 1811, were a case in point. Starving men set out to destroy machinery which they said was destroying their livelihoods. They claimed to be led by a Ned Ludd whose office was said to be in Sherwood Forest. Whether he really existed or not is still unknown. The response of Parliament was violent. A Bill was rushed through making machine-breaking a capital offence despite such an act being already punishable by 14 years' transportation. Only Lord Byron in the House of Lords made any serious opposition.

---

2.   *Speeches.* ii. 287-8. 1838.

Suppose one of these men, he said, as I have seen them
- meagre with famine, sullen with despair, careless of
a life which your lordships are perhaps about to value
at something less than the price of a stocking-frame -
suppose this man (and there are a thousand such from
whom you may select your victims) dragged into court
to be tried for this new offence by this new law, still
there are two things wanting to convict and condemn
him; and these are, in my opinion, 12 butchers for a
jury and a Jeffreys for a Judge.

A Jeffreys there may not have been but hundreds of
people, including young boys, were hanged or transported.
One woman of 54 was sentenced to death for helping to
force dealers to sell bread, butter and cheese below their
normal price. Before long the riots subsided but the
supposed insurrection had never been a possibility except
in the fevered imaginations of government Ministers.

The following years saw a continuation of repression,
with the "Peterloo Massacre" and Sidmouth's notorious
"Six Acts". These Acts were rushed through a frightened
Parliament and gave magistrates powers to prevent
meetings and search private houses. They also forbade
drillings, and processions with bands or banners. They
made publishers of "blasphemous and seditious libels"
liable to imprisonment or transportation and imposed a
tax of fourpence a copy on all newspapers and pamphlets
in order to reduce the circulation of those opposed to the
government.

Economic distress was still widespread, however, in
1830 when, for four months, agricultural labourers
revolted under the leadership of "Captain Swing" against
the introduction of new threshing machinery that
threatened their livelihoods. Although many of those
arrested had done no more than attend a meeting they
were charged before Special Commissions which were set

up for the sole purpose of trying them. Apparently the local and county magistrates could not be counted upon to find the men guilty. They were charged with breaking machinery, rioting or conspiring to raise wages. In the event 252 were sentenced to death (of whom 19 were hanged), over 500 were transported and over 600 sent to prison.

Since legal agitation had become difficult some radicals turned to conspiracy, although the Cato Street plot to assassinate the entire Cabinet in 1820 was government controlled.[3] On the other hand, important figures such as Sir Robert Peel, Fowell Buxton and Henry Brougham had taken up the mantle of Romilly and there had emerged a new industrial-based middle class whose aspirations for reform were voiced by James Mill and Bentham. Mill, for example, in his *Essay on Government*[4] in 1818, launched a violent attack on the unfitness of the aristocracy to govern and proclaimed the middle class to be the highest product of civilization. Brougham also championed the clamour for power of the middle class, telling the House of Lords on October 7, 1831, "by the people I mean the middle classes, the wealth and intelligence of the country, the glory of the British name."[5]

So far as the criminal law was concerned the middle class wanted to replace the discretion so beloved by the aristocracy with certainty in punishment and a reduction in the incidence of the death penalty. For example, more than 1,000 bankers petitioned Parliament to abolish capital punishment for forgery because its very severity often prevented the prosecution and punishment of

---

3.   *Cf.* John Hostettler. *Thomas Wakley. An Improbable Radical.* 22-30. 1993.
4.   *Encyclopedia Britannica.* Supplement.
5.   *Speeches. Op. cit.* 617.

criminals. Similar petitions from other groups flowed in until Brougham exclaimed that "the table groaned with them."[6]

What they all wanted was a better protection of their property and more efficient laws. After all, even if a prosecution took place for any felony that attracted capital punishment the jury would often be anxious to avoid the penalty of death unless violence had been used. On theft in particular we may quote Blackstone's well-known words: "the mercy of juries often made them strain a point, and bring in larceny to be under the value of twelvepence, when it was really of much greater value ... A kind of *pious perjury*."[7] In many cases the difference between the real value of an article and that accepted by the jury was quite startling.

Nevertheless, the philosophy for changing the criminal law came from Bentham. In the words of John Stuart Mill he "gave voice to the interests and instincts [of the middle class], he is the great subversive thinker of his age and country."[8] We shall presently look at the work for reform of Peel, Brougham and others. But, although Bentham inspired and encouraged them, he was unreasoning in his contempt for their attempts to achieve what was politically possible in reducing cruelty and injustice rather than getting bogged down in his all-embracing schemes. Of Peel, he told John Bowring, his biographer, "Peel is weak and feeble ... he has done all the good he is capable of doing and that is but little."[9] And of Brougham's eloquent and successful speech on law reform to the House of Commons on February 7, 1828, which he delivered over six hours whilst sucking oranges, Bentham

---

6   *Hansard.* 1830. vol.24. col.1058.

7.   *Op. cit.* 248.

8.   Bentham. *London and Westminster Review* 469. (August 1838).

9.   *Memoirs of Jeremy Bentham.* 594.

commented, two days later: "Mr. Brougham's mountain is delivered, and behold! - the mouse."[10]

Bentham studied and exposed in great detail the obscurity of the law, its complexity and expense, as well as its artificiality and irrationality. He proposed to codify the substantive, procedural and penal laws for all the countries of the world. On punishments he was totally opposed to the death penalty and he rejected the feudal concepts of felony, deodands, benefit of clergy, outlawry and the consequences of suicide. He accepted Beccaria's principles but subjected the penal law to a far more searching and extensive inquiry.

To Bentham all punishment was in itself evil since it inflicted pain. It was a counter-crime committed with the authority of the law. It was to be permitted only in so far as it promised to exclude some greater evil.[11] Punishments had to be directed to both specific and general deterrence. This was achieved by taking away from the offender the physical power of repeating his offence, or the desire to, or by making him and others afraid of offending. These objects, together with rehabilitation in prison, were the only justification of punishments.

Bentham wanted law to be an efficient instrument of social control and this led him into inconsistency on the question of torture. He accepted the justice of Beccaria's observations on torture but thought there could be occasions when it might be used that Beccaria had not considered. In thinking of torture solely as pain inflicted on the body he thought it could replace other punishments which caused greater hardship. Furthermore, it might more easily achieve its purpose and could instantly be made to cease. He was particularly

---

10.   *Ibid.* 588.
11.   *Rationale of Punishment.* 1830.

concerned where the fate of large numbers of people, or the state, were concerned.

Professor Twining has given a modern example to explain Bentham's position. "It is believed that an atomic bomb has been placed somewhere in a major city with a timing device attached to it. X, who is believed to have information about the location of this bomb, has been captured."[12] Nevertheless, it seems clear that Beccaria's appeal to principles of justice and humanity were subsumed by Bentham's insistence on logic on this occasion.

On the other hand, we cannot diminish the significance of Bentham's influence for good on law reform. Peel called him the "sage of the law" and Sir Henry Maine claimed, "I do not know a single law reform effected since Bentham's day which cannot be traced to his influence."[13] As to his views on the death penalty, transportation, and imprisonment we shall examine them as we come upon these issues shortly.

Sir Robert Peel

The first serious steps on the road to reform of the penal law came when Sir Robert Peel, who was born in 1788 and educated at Blackburn Grammar School, Harrow and Oxford, was Home Secretary from 1822 to 1827 in succession to Sidmouth. It is true that some reforms had already been effected, such as the abolition of the whipping of women in 1820. Peel wanted to go further, however, and in particular reduce the incidence of capital punishment. He was to tell the House of Commons in

---

12.   Bentham on Torture. *Northern Ireland Legal Quarterly*. No.3, vol.24. 305 (Autumn 1973).
13.   *Early History of Institutions*. 397. 1875.

1830 that, "it is impossible to conceal from ourselves that capital punishments are more frequent and the criminal law more severe on the whole in this country than in any country in the world." "I propose," he declared, "to break this sleep of a century," referring to the past lack of substantial progress on reform. He ensured that the Waltham Black Act was repealed and that the dangerous farce of benefit of clergy was abolished. He then persuaded the government to examine the whole question of criminal law in the knowledge that if he were to reduce the number of capital offences further something would have to be done to improve the scope and efficiency of secondary punishments, including imprisonment.

People still found it difficult to conceive of a real alternative to the punishment of death for felonies and Peel himself wrote a letter to Sydney Smith on March 24, 1826 in which he admitted that "the whole subject of what is called secondary punishment is full of difficulty ... I despair of any remedy but that which I wish I could hope for - a great reduction in the amount of crime."[14]

He did attempt, however, to deal with the evils of the prison system and secured the enactment of the Gaol Act of 1823. This made mandatory John Howard's four principles of providing secure and sanitary accommodation, making gaolers salaried servants of the local authorities, instituting a regime of reformation, and ensuring systematic inspection of all prisons by visiting justices. Unfortunately, although the Act had some persuasive effect, there was no central machinery available to enforce it.

Despite the difficulties, however, he produced four measures between 1827 and 1830 which dealt with larceny, forgery, malicious injury to property and offences against the person. Between them they consolidated over

---

14.   C.S. Parker. *Sir Robert Peel from his Private Correspondence.* i. 402.

200 statutes and severely reduced the number of capital offences. With these achievements Peel felt he had gone as far as public opinion would allow, at least on the death penalty, and henceforth he opposed the successful campaign of William Ewart, MP, to secure a further reduction in the number of capital offences. Bentham merely remarked, in a letter to Daniel O'Connell dated July 15, 1828, "Mr. Peel is for consolidation in contradistinction to codification: I am for codification in contradistinction to consolidation."[15]

Peel was being pragmatic, testing how far he could go if he were not to be defeated as Romilly had been. As a consequence he underestimated how far public opinion had changed, and was continuing to change. In the end he could have gone further, but he broke the mould and others continued what he had started, in spite of his opposition. Nonetheless, notwithstanding his valuable contribution to ameliorating the effects of many punishments, Peel did allow the use of whipping to be extended and he made no effort separately to improve the lot of young offenders.

Juvenile Offenders

We may pause at this point to reflect upon the terrifying plight of juveniles in the nineteenth century and before.[16] Young people, including children, were treated no differently from adults when it came to punishments. Even for trivial offences they could be hanged, sent to the Hulks or transported for many years.

For example, on January 18, 1801, *The Times*, reported that an urchin of 13 named Andrew Brunning was

---

15.   Bowring. *Op. cit.* 595.
16.   Much of the material here was published in an article by the author in *Justice of the Peace*, vol.156. Nos.22, 23 (May/June, 1992).

sentenced to death for stealing a spoon from a house. Greville recorded seeing several boys sentenced to be hanged and remarked, "never did I see boys cry so." And the poet Rogers saw a "cartload of young girls, in dresses of various colours, on their way to be hanged at Tyburn Tree."[17]

Reform was impeded by a general lack of understanding that children should be treated more mercifully and also by the perceived increase in juvenile crime at the time. Even the reforming MP Fowell Buxton, in a speech famous for its impassioned plea for reform of the criminal law as a means of reducing crime, told the House of Commons on May 23, 1821, that in London alone there were from 8,000 to 10,000 children earning their daily bread by their daily misdeeds, living by petty pilfering, and growing into serious criminals![18]

Others too, believed harsh law bred crime. In 1815 a *Society for Investigating the Causes of the Alarming Increase of Juvenile Delinquency in the Metropolis* had been founded by Peter Bradford, the "Spitalfield Philanthropist." Included on its Committee were Dr. Stephen Lushington, Fowell Buxton, James Mill and David Ricardo. In their view the causes of delinquency were the severity of the criminal law, the mixing of children with "atrocious" adult criminals in prisons and the defective state of the police. They wanted to see much imprisonment and corporal punishment replaced by "... mildness of persuasion and gentleness of reproof ..."[19]

This approach led, in 1821, to a Bill for the Punishment, Correction and Reform of Young Persons. It provided that, instead of committing children to prison to await trial at Quarter Sessions, or even Assizes, for

---

17.   Quoted in L.A. Parry: *History of Torture*. 15. 1933.
18.   *Hansard*. May 23, 1821. vol.5. col.903.
19.   *Report*. 26-7. (1816).

such petty offences as stealing apples or tarts, they should be dealt with summarily by two justices with a view to their reform. Unfortunately, it received insufficient support and was defeated.

A similar proposal was made in 1828 by the Select Committee on Criminal Law[20] which had concluded that lengthy imprisonment awaiting trial was degrading and led to vice. Again, however, nothing was done since the authorities, including many JPs, although concerned at the increase in juvenile crime, felt little disquiet at the awful punishments inflicted upon a very large number of young children and saw no process of cause and effect.

Then, in 1833, following the Reform Act of the previous year, Lord Chancellor Brougham secured the appointment of a Royal Commission enjoined to bring about a fundamental reform of the country's archaic criminal law.[21] Among the particular questions the Commissioners were asked to consider was the desirability of distinguishing the modes of trial of juvenile and adult offenders. The main issue still remained whether greater use should be made of summary trial to avoid lengthy periods of imprisonment on remand and to secure lighter sentences.

The Commissioners decided to question witnesses before preparing their report. The replies given to them by the generally enlightened men they approached are surprising. They reveal some compassion but a startlingly hard-headed attitude to young offenders, including small children. The evils of the existing system were deplored but by no means all the witnesses agreed the system should be changed.

---

20. *P.P.* VI. 12. (1828).
21. For a study of this Royal Commission and its successors *cf.* John Hostettler. *The Politics of Criminal Law: Reform in the Nineteenth Century.* 1992.

Richard Mayne, a young barrister recently appointed Commissioner of the Metropolitan Police by Sir Robert Peel, considered existing punishments were often too short and neither deterred nor reformed juvenile offenders. They should be particularly increased, he said, where, even though proof of larceny was not complete, the accused were convicted under the Police Act as *reputed* thieves and *suspected* persons (my italics).

Mayne found the right to search at night extremely valuable and wished to have it extended to searching houses such as the "Finish" in Covent Garden, low saloons and penny theatres. And, if a youth with no obvious means of getting his "bread" was seen about the streets, there should be some means of confining him or preventing him going about to do mischief.

Alderman Harmer, a very successful defence attorney and well-known penal reformer, also gave evidence to the Commissioners. He had seen, he said, little children sent for trial suffer a terrible ordeal. Subsequently, they could not retrieve their character and would often become criminals. He, therefore, advocated summary punishment by two magistrates. Slight punishments like flogging with a birch, such as schoolmasters often gave, or solitary confinement for a day or two, would be suitable.

Of course, such witnesses, of which there were many more, were products of their time and either thought harsh treatment was desirable or wished to ameliorate the law without going too far and becoming "soft". Others had more vision, however, and saw the improving effects on both children and society of a more humane approach.

For example, Sir Eardley Wilmot, magistrate for the County of Warwick, concluded that the main reason for the great increase in crime was the early imprisonment of children. He recommended immediate and summary review of offences committed by the young to avoid the stigma and contamination of imprisonment and the publicity of trial. Larceny by the young should be made a minor offence, to be dealt with by two magistrates with power to punish or discharge without punishment, rather than put a child who stole a bun into gaol for three months on remand.

Dr. Lushington, in his evidence to the Commissioners, strongly opposed corporal punishment. In his experience, for larceny to the amount of a few pence, a first offender would often receive from a month to three months' imprisonment and hard labour, sometimes with whipping or solitary confinement. As a result, children could end up in a state horrible to contemplate. And it produced no benefit or good at all - only callousness.

Mr. George Warry, a magistrate at Bridgewater, was also concerned that a young accused awaiting trial was often imprisoned for many weeks imbibing corruption. Extensive machinery was set in motion to deal with trifling cases - "like a steam-engine - to crush a fly." And a too frequent use of the criminal courts tended to a prostitution of the dignity of the law. He also favoured a more summary proceeding. It is interesting that no one (apart from the Commissioners) appeared to consider that the use of bail might ease some of the problems. Perhaps there was insufficient policing for the idea to be attractive.

1847 Select Committee

It is useful to compare the replies given by the Commissioners' witnesses with a few of those given to a House of Lords Select Committee set up in 1847 to inquire into the law regarding juvenile offenders and transportation.[22] The picture revealed of the treatment of young offenders remains appalling.

22.　*PP.* VIII. 2 Reports (1847).

Lord Brougham took the chair at the committee and the first witness was Charles Ewan Law, QC, Recorder of London. A great many children under the age of 12, he said, had been convicted of felony before him. Incredibly, he had sent some to the Hulks, disused warships used as prisons well-known for their appalling living conditions. Others had been sentenced to three years' imprisonment, despite his adding that he thought simple larceny should be made a misdemeanour.

Another witness, John Adams, a Judge and Chairman of the Middlesex Sessions from 1836 to 1844, had often tried boys under 15 years of age. In a burst of anti-semitism, he blamed "the Jews", since anything children would steal they took from them in return for a few pence. At first the children would spend the money on "... gingerbread, cakes etc., they next became frequenters of penny theatres ... and are trained until they become thieves." Similarly, M.D. Hill, Recorder of Birmingham, claimed that he tried as many boys and girls under 16 as amounted to a quarter of all other ages together who appeared before him.

Captain Hall, the Governor of Parkhurst Prison, indicated that he took in all ages from 10 to 18. He claimed that the reformatory regime was educational and it appeared that almost all his boys worked out part of their sentence for two or three years before being transported. Nearly all the witnesses agreed that transportation could not be abandoned, since it invoked a terror greater than all other punishments except death. They also thought that imprisonment was not an efficient punishment, even with hard labour and separation or silence, since it had no deterrent effect after a second sentence. And for young first offenders, it resulted in a fatal contamination so that one saw a frightful picture of boys under 12 returning within three or four years as often as 15 times, and on average nine.

The committee concluded, therefore, that young first offenders should be sent to reformatory asylums on the principle of Parkhurst. As with the later borstals, the sentences were made longer to permit training. Indeed, there was almost unanimity among the witnesses in their opposition to short sentences and, contrary to the view of Parliament, for the retention of capital punishment for a variety of offences.

Government Failure

To return to the Commissioners, they gave their usual meticulous consideration to all the evidence and points of view available and presented their report on March 10, 1837.[23] They came to the conclusion that the principal distinction in the mode of trial between adults and juveniles should be an increase in the summary jurisdiction of magistrates which they thought would materially diminish juvenile crime. It was a proposal of great significance.

They suggested that upon charges of larceny of property to the value of 10 shillings, where the age of the culprit did not exceed 15 years, a single JP should have a discretionary power to dismiss the prisoner altogether if the circumstances of the offence were trivial. Alternatively, he could take sureties for good behaviour or bail the prisoner until trial. In other cases, two justices sitting together should have greater summary powers to avoid imprisonment on remand for those under 16.

It might be argued, said the Commissioners, that the constitutional form of trial by jury had to be preserved. The practical question, however, was whether the advantage gained by the diminution of imprisonment on remand in the case of young persons was not cheaply

---

23.   *PP.* XXXI. (1837).

purchased by the sacrifice of the benefit to be derived from their trial by jury. Considering the simplicity and trivial nature of the offences in question, they thought their investigation by a jury was unnecessary.

Committal of a child over seven for trial at Assizes or Quarter Sessions where he would spend weeks or months in prison awaiting trial produced positive evils, especially in the destruction of morals, with no counter-balancing advantages. The formality of a solemn trial in such (often trivial) cases, derogated from the dignity of a superior court of justice and did not deter. The slightness of the offence and youth of the offender usually rendered him an object of compassion, and if the jury did not acquit him altogether, they would recommend mercy and the sentence would be little more than nominal.

As a result, neither of the two great objects of penal laws, the prevention of crime and the reformation of the criminal, were accomplished. Indeed, said the Commissioners with a mixture of compassion and realism, where a theft resulted only from incitement by others, it might often be less mischievous to society to pass over the offence altogether.

In the event, the government refused to implement the report it had sought. Sir Eardley Wilmot pressed it to do so but Lord John Russell, the Home Secretary, declined on the ground that it would violate the principle of trial by jury.[24]

However, the work of the Commissioners and the committee did come to fruition in 1847 when the Juvenile Offenders Act[25] was passed and when an Act of 1854 established reformatory schools for the "better care and reformation of youthful offenders." The 1847 Act gave magistrates increased powers to deal summarily with

---

24.   *Hansard.* April 1837. Vol.37, col.926.
25.   10 and 11 Vict. c.82.

juveniles so that an offender under 14 guilty of simple larceny could be whipped, or discharged without punishment.

No further substantial improvement in the law was now to be achieved before the end of the century. However, the age limit of the 1847 Act was raised to 16 by the Juvenile Offenders Act of 1850.[26] Prior to its enactment this Act was bitterly attacked by the *Law Magazine*, the journal of the Bar, in an article entitled "The Bill Against Trials by Jury."[27]

It argued that giving magistrates power to convict summarily removed at least 50 per cent of criminal cases from trial by jury, "... a large, perilous and unconstitutional inroad on that noble institution." Furthermore, the new power to give sentences as short as three months was "preposterous mockery", since it gave no time for reformation of the criminal. Totally incensed, the magazine finally erupted: "we are really at a loss how to grapple with a Bill so outrageously silly as this." Yet simple larcenies remained felonies and indictable, the statutes merely enabling them to be tried summarily if the accused agreed. The real effect was to relieve pressure on Quarter Sessions and to increase greatly the number of larcenies tried.

Nonetheless, however falteringly, a step forward had been taken towards the more sympathetic and discriminating treatment of young offenders that was ultimately to lead to the statutes relating to children and juveniles to which we give effect today.

---

26.   13 & 14 Vict. c.37.
27.   42. 155. (1849).

CHAPTER 9

CENTURY OF REFORM

The Crusade Against the Death Penalty

We have seen that capital punishment had been a central element in the criminal law throughout the centuries. By the nineteenth century our penal laws were the most sanguinary in Europe, as Peel had recognized. But a significant movement against this "bloody code" was growing in England, fuelled by Beccaria's concept that the death penalty was a war by the state against those whose destruction it considered necessary.

Bentham, for his part, argued that capital punishment was undesirable since, *inter alia:*

1. It could not be used for compensation as its source was destroyed.
2. Executed men could not be reformed.
3. The death penalty was unequal since men were unequal and it was not variable or remissible. Judges were not infallible and many innocent victims had perished.

Romilly had followed Bentham's lead and by the 1820s Peel had acted to some extent and, despite his failure to see it, a growing tide of public opinion was becoming insistent for change. Influential magazines such as the *Edinburgh Review* and the *Quarterly Review* clamoured for reform and were joined by the *Morning Herald* and *Morning Chronicle* newspapers. Horace Walpole, Dr. Johnson and Oliver Goldsmith had also helped change the climate of opinion with their condemnations of the Tyburn shambles as a national disgrace. Also bitterly condemned was the practice of allowing gaolers to charge a fee to allow members of the public to enter a prison and gaze at condemned criminals during their last hours.

The Tyburn Tree, used as a gallows on which some 24 victims could be hanged simultaneously, was to be found at the corner of Edgware Road in London where the Marble Arch now stands. It was first used as long ago as the reign of Richard I and by the eighteenth century its influence was so malign that in 1783 it was abolished by the Fox-North Coalition. Public hanging was transferred to Newgate where it was thought the prisoners incarcerated there might be deterred from crime, as well as the general public.

Prior to that year the prisoners due to meet the public hangman had been taken from Newgate to Tyburn in a grim procession accompanied by either jeering or applauding crowds. Wealthy prisoners often proceeded in their own coaches with a hearse bringing up the rear. Poorer convicts usually sat on a coffin in the hearse. Some prisoners managed to retain their dignity; others were a more pitiful sight. All were offered a glass of ale when the procession stopped at the Hospital of St. Giles in the Fields and, when that was closed down, at "The Bowl" - a nearby public house. Both the processions and the hangings on Tyburn Tree were gruesome spectacles and the poet William Blake was appalled by some he witnessed when as a child he lived in Stratford Place near

Tyburn.[1]

A reduction in the use of capital punishment had become a burning question of great political significance during the eighteenth and early nineteenth centuries. Thomas Carlyle was to put the view of the minority who favoured retention of the death penalty with a thunderous outpouring when he wrote:

> We ... dare not allow thee to continue longer among us. As a palpable deserter ... fighting thus against the whole Universe and its Laws, we send thee back into the whole Universe, solemnly expel thee from our community; and will in the name of God, not with joy and exaltation, but with sorrows stern as thy own, hang thee on Wednesday next, and so end ... "Revenge," my friends! revenge, and the natural hatred of scoundrels and the ineradicable tendency to ... pay them what they had merited: this is forevermore intrinsically a correct, and even a divine, feeling in the mind of every man.[2]

But, after all, Carlyle had also written an outrageous panegyric about the wonderland atmosphere of a prison he actually visited in 1849, as part of his campaign against the introduction of penitentiaries.

Peel, for his part, had put the weight of the Home Office behind reform until he thought he had gone far enough for public opinion. And when the irrepressible William Ewart introduced a Bill on March 27, 1832, to repeal capital punishment for stealing in a dwellinghouse to the value of £5 and for horse, sheep and cattle stealing

---

1. "Milton". Blake's *Poems & Prophecies*. 113. (1927). *Cf.* also Jonathan Swift. *Poetical Works*. i. 202. (1833).
2. *Latter-Day Pamphlets*. 66, 67. 1872.

Peel intervened no less than three times in the debate, asserting that the proposal was a "most dangerous experiment." Despite this and fierce opposition in the House of Lords the Bill was passed, but only after a compromise whereby the death penalty was replaced by one punishment only, namely transportation for life.

By the 1820s the main issues involved had become the inhumanity of the sheer number of capital statutes, the question whether the death penalty was effective as a deterrent and necessary at all, and the effect of the uncertainty of punishment caused by the arbitrary selection of only a proportion of those convicted to be executed. All these features and assumptions were encouraged by the ruling aristocracy as a means of upholding their rule and legitimacy, particularly in the shires. But now the industrial middle class had its own reasons for demanding more rational and effective punishments. Naturally it desired more efficient protection for its own type of property, but it also wanted to see a reformed criminal-law system as part of a more utilitarian and humane society.

Piecemeal reform was not sufficient. Peel had been wrong about public opinion. Throughout the country there sprang up committees and societies to enlighten the populace about the issues involved. Petitions flowed into Parliament and meetings for reform were packed out. Journals and newspapers entered the fray and at a public meeting held at the Exeter Hall in London on May 30, 1831, addressed by Dr. Lushington, a typical resolution was passed calling on Parliament to give attention to the punishment of death which was "at variance with justice, religion and the feelings of the nation."

Invoking the name of Bentham one writer argued that in England,

. . . law grinds the poor, rich men make law. Here is the secret of our bloody code - of the perverse ingenuity by which its abominations have so long been defended; "whoso stealeth a sheep, let him die the death," says the statute: could so monstrous a law have been enacted had our legislators been chosen by the people of England? But our lawmakers hitherto have been our landlords. By the sale of his sheep, the farmer pays his rent; by the rent of the farmer, the luxury of the Member is upheld; touch one link touch all.[3]

Another reformer invoked Beccaria. It was not enough, he wrote, to know which punishment inspired the greatest degree of terror. If that punishment which excited the greatest fear was necessarily the best then it would be necessary to use breaking upon the wheel, burning alive, boiling alive and disembowelling alive. This was not done, he continued, because the brutalizing effects of such horrible spectacles upon public morals produced an evil so great as to outweigh their direct advantages. Like the death penalty they also suffered from being transient as examples and irremissible.[4]

With the enactment of the Reform Act the Whigs and the middle class found their opportunity. Within a year the Criminal Law Commissioners were appointed to reform and codify the criminal law. Their second report[5] contained all the evidence they had obtained on the death penalty from witnesses together with their conclusions and proposals. It was a skilful analysis of the case for abolition for most crimes. Soon after it was published the Home Secretary, Lord John Russell, wrote a letter to the

---

3.   H.B. Andrews. *Criminal Law: Being a Commentary on Bentham on Death Punishment.* 1833.
4.   Thomas Wrightson. *On the Punishment of Death.* 3rd edn. 1837.
5.   *PP.* XXXVI. 138 (1836).

Commissioners, on September 19, 1836, asking for their assistance in preparing a Bill on capital punishment.[6]

In the letter he also put his own point of view that public opinion was unlikely to accept the abolition of capital punishment in cases of burglary or robbery with violence, and that the shedding of a man's blood by premeditated violence could not cease to be capital without increasing the number of such crimes. Although he did not say so Russell was clearly anticipating difficulties in the House of Lords and was anxious to avoid a backlash from the aristocracy.

However, armed with the Commissioners' drafts, Russell introduced the Bill into the House of Commons.[7] It provided for the removal of the death penalty from 21 of the 37 offences still capital, and for restrictions in the use of such punishment in the 16 remaining. It was speedily enacted and proved a fitting climax to the crusade for reform commenced by Romilly. As a measure of its success, in 1831 over 1,600 people were sentenced to death, although many were not executed. By 1838 the number sentenced was reduced to 116.

During the debate William Ewart had proposed an Amendment to remove capital punishment from all offences except murder, in place of Russell's 21 crimes. Despite Lord John's opposition Ewart lost by only one vote. Such strong support expressed the desire of the newly enfranchised middle class for a more substantial reduction in the use of capital punishment as part of its general endeavour to reduce crime and extend the work-ethic in a fast-expanding industrial economy. It was an important aspect of the movement for general reform of the criminal law - itself an integral element in the powerful changes taking place in English society at the

---

6.   *PP.* XXXI. 31 (1837).
7.   *Hansard* (1837) vol.37. col.709.

time. In the event the death penalty was soon to be inflicted only in cases of murder and treason.

Secondary Punishments

We have seen how Peel, in a letter to Sydney Smith, saw the need for satisfactory alternative punishments to the death penalty for serious crimes, but failed to conceive what they could be. Imprisonment was still not regarded as suitable, which is not surprising considering the lack of prisons available and the deplorable state of those that did exist. And both the Hulks and transportation were abhorred by all liberal-minded people.

The Hulks

As a consequence of the War of Independence, from 1776 prisoners could no longer be transported to North America. As a temporary alternative many convicts were sent to two prison Hulks, the *Censor* and the *Justitia*, which were rotting, disused warships moored in the Thames at Woolwich. Conditions aboard were appalling with a pitiful diet including putrid meat and mouldy biscuits. To house the increasing number of convicts who could not be transported, further Hulks were later established at Plymouth, Portsmouth, Chatham and Sheerness.

In 1847 Thomas Duncombe, one of two radical MPs for Finsbury, sent a statement to *The Times,* in which he accused the superintendent of convicts, J.H. Capper, of gross neglect of duty and mismanagement of the Hulks. Capper denied the charges but a prison inspector was appointed to inquire into the position at Woolwich. Although the inspector dismissed some of Duncombe's specific charges, his 29-page report and the evidence he received were devastating.[8]

Even on the hospital ship the diet caused scurvy and the oatmeal was so bad that the patients threw it overboard. The great majority of the patients were infested with vermin. The earnings of the prisoners, who worked on building the Royal Arsenal at Woolwich, were mismanaged and lunatics were confined with the other prisoners. One insane inmate was flogged. It was found that the assistant-surgeon was not a qualified surgeon at all but a student. Cleanliness was non-existent and the brutal life on the Hulks was described as "Hell on Earth." So grim was the report that the government was forced to take action and the Hulks were gradually phased out of use but only after a life of some 80 years during which they had held tens of thousands of prisoners in such wretched conditions.

Transportation

We have witnessed how those found guilty at the "Bloody Assize" but not executed were sold as slaves in the West Indies. Earlier, in 1615, a Privy Council Order had permitted the sending of criminals to America which was also the fate of many vagrants. Such transportation was normally an alternative to hanging. Between 1655 and 1699, 4,500 convicted felons and vagrants suffered this fate. Merchants were paid by the government for each journey and on arrival, usually at the plantations in Virginia, each convict was sold to the highest bidder. Negro slaves from Africa were to prove cheaper, however, and in 1776 the Declaration of Independence put an end to transportation to North America.

The government at Westminster tried to resolve the

---

8.   831. XLVIII. (1847).

consequent crisis by packing more convicts into the Hulks. However, this only created more problems than it solved since the Hulks had a limited capacity. In the 1780s, therefore, Pitt settled for a penal colony to be established in New South Wales. This was favoured as securing the removal of criminals from English society and because of its allegedly low budget. As a result, between 1788 and 1853, 152,170 convicts were sent, out of whom 149,507 arrived.[9] Death was not the only terror, however. On the journey, convicts were confined, ill-fed, kept in irons and rarely allowed on deck. On arrival, large numbers were found to be unable to walk or even move a hand or a foot. Once put to work, if they were idle they suffered up to 500 lashes and were kept in double irons if so ordered by a magistrate.[10]

Transportation could be for seven, 10 or 14 years or for life, and A.G.L. Shaw records that some three-fifths of all convicts were transported after 1830.[11] Those imposing the penalty seem to have had little idea of what was involved for the unfortunate victim. As we have seen, Lord Ellenborough, for example, in standing firm for the retention of the death penalty claimed that transportation was "only a summer airing by an easy migration to a milder climate."[12]

Bentham, on the other hand, was totally opposed to this form of punishment and regarded it as a complete failure. He thought it resulted, at an enormous expense of money, labour and suffering, in the foundation of a community basically vicious and miserable and growing every year more depraved and more wretched. It could hardly be said to be exemplary, so great was the

---

9.   A.G.L. Shaw. *Convicts & the Colonies*. Appendix. 1966.
10. *Ibid.* 72, 108.
11. *Ibid.* 148.
12. *Ante.* 111.

disproportion between the real and apparent suffering. The community in England saw a convict sent on a long voyage to a fertile country with a fine climate. That was the example. The reality was that, after rotting in the Hulks for a year or two, the miserable wretch was crammed with hundreds of others into the floating prison in which he faced the risks of famine, disease and death, only to reach a life of slavery, suffering and misery.

In a letter dated August 9, 1802, Bentham wrote to Charles Bunbury of the "utter repugnance" with which he viewed Botany Bay.[13] The next day he presented him with a long summary of his comments covering several large pages in tabulated columns under the title: *Panopticon* v. *New South Wales, August 10, 1802.*[14] After long lists of objections to transportation he concluded that its real purpose was incapacitation by mere distance and that it could involve little deterrence and no reformation. He was also disturbed that, unlike his projected Panopticon prison, it necessarily resulted in a severe lack of control so that there was no check on forbidden practices.

Shaw, in contrast, thinks that transportation offered what seemed the only alternative to capital punishment and, although finally abandoned as insufficiently deterrent, it provided an essential means of punishment at a time when the unreformed gaols made long terms of imprisonment virtually impossible.[15] In the end, transportation to New South Wales was suspended in 1840, to Van Dieman's Land in 1846 and Australia finally closed its doors in 1867. Thus ended this mockery of moral justice.

---

13. *BM. Add.Mss.* 33109. f.331.
14. *Ibid. Cf.* Letter to Lord Pelham under the same title on December 17, 1802. *Works.* iv. 173-248. The Panopticon was a startling idea for a prison dreamed up by Bentham of which more later.
15. *Op. cit.* 360.

Imprisonment

For enlightened people such as Bentham, who could see nothing but evil in both the death penalty and transportation, some alternative had to be found for those sentenced to long terms of punishment. And his views aroused wide support. The commercial and manufacturing middle class wanted a more efficient deterrent to crimes such as theft and forgery than the capricious use of the punitive Game Laws and the death penalty so beloved of the aristocracy. General opposition to the brutality of hanging, the Hulks and transportation was also widespread. The growth of crime in large urban and industrial centres was creating a new urgency for deterrent punishment and policing.

Sir Archibald Alison, the Sheriff of Lanarkshire, claimed that two million people had been brought together in the manufacturing towns in a space of 40 years, an astonishing migration without precedent in history. This had led to destitution, profligacy, sensuality, crime and insurrections advancing with unheard of rapidity.[16] What was needed was a new system of penalties to fit the crime and the establishment of an organized, regular police force.

After transportation to North America had ceased so abruptly the government had appointed a Commission of three, including John Howard, to consider the long-term future treatment of prisoners. Their recommendations were incorporated in the Penitentiary Act of 1779. A number of "Penitentiary Houses" were to be built in order to teach an honest and industrious way of life by means of hard labour and solitary confinement. There would also be religious instruction to implant sobriety, cleanliness and hygiene. In the event the Act became submerged

---

16. *Blackwood's Edinburgh Magazine.* vol.56. 1-14. July 1844.

under Pitt's conversion to the penal colony of New South Wales. Only two penitentiaries were built, one at Gloucester and the other at Southwell.

Bentham, meanwhile, was considering the possibility of analogy between crimes and punishments.[17] Analogy, he wrote, was a method of punishment for "doing to a delinquent the same hurt he has done to another." Well, not quite the same hurt apparently. Thus an arsonist who caused death should suffer from fire, but not to an extent to cause his own death. A person who drowned another was himself to be drowned, but in such a manner that he could be restored to life. And a poisoner was to be poisoned, but only symbolically as remedies were to be at hand for use after a suitable interval.[18]

Even genius has its lapses and Bentham was hoping that the threat of such uncivilized punishments would appeal to the imagination without inflicting serious injury, even possibly avoiding the necessity of their use. This would hardly be likely when it became known that the ultimate sanction was not to be used and the *Edinburgh Review,* which generally supported Bentham, sensibly thought his idea of giving such punishments an appearance of harshness which was to be absent in practice would bring the law into ridicule and contempt.[19] But a century later, Stephen, in approving flogging, wrote that a man who cruelly inflicted pain on another should be made to feel what it was like, and that it should be severe and not like a birching at a public school.[20] And it may be noted that analogy, or "mirror punishment," was practised in Holland in the seventeenth

---

17. *Cf. The Rationale of Punishment.* c.8. Written in 1775, this work was published in Paris in 1811 and in London only in 1830.
18. *MSS.* University College Library. fol.96. f.10.
19. Vol.22. 11. (1813).
20. *Op. cit.* ii. 91.

and eighteenth centuries.[21]

Bentham himself must have had doubts, however, because he also wrote that "if in other respects any particular mode of punishment be eligible, analogy alone is not a sufficient recommendation. The value of this property amounts to very little," he added, "because even in the case of murder other punishments may be devised the analogy of which will be sufficiently striking."

Perhaps widespread analogy was something Stephen had in mind when he said that some of Bentham's ideas were like "unexploded shells, buried under the ruins which they have made." Although he did later observe that Bentham's practical influence upon the legislation of his own and other countries was comparable only to that of Adam Smith upon commerce.

Bentham then turned to inquire whether the use of imprisonment could be extended by making it more effective and cheaper. He now conjured up a novel type of prison to be called the Panopticon or "Inspection House". This was to be distinguished by three striking new features. First, from the form of the building, a circular iron and glass cage, the governor would be able to see each prisoner (and gaoler) at all times without being seen by them and could direct them without leaving his post. "The spider in his web," exclaimed Edmund Burke.

Secondly, the management of the prison was to be carried on by contract. The government would pay a fixed price for the total expense of each convict and, in return, the contractor would have the profit after a proportion had been paid to the convict. This would replace the existing system of fees paid to gaolers by the prisoners.

Thirdly, all accounts would be available for public inspection and the prison open at all times to every

---

21.   For examples *cf.* P. Spierensburg. *Op. cit.* 73.

magistrate, and at certain hours to the public generally. The cost factor was of primary importance. Transportation was costing over £1 million every 10 years, approximately £38 for each convict. Under Bentham's contract, each convict was to cost the government 13s. 10d. including 1s. 10d. for the building and land. Also included would be a fund to indemnify persons injured in the course of the convicts' crimes.

Although Parliament agreed to this cyclopic monster in 1794, it was never built at the Millbank site purchased for it where the Tate Gallery now stands. One was built in America, however, and another at Breda in Holland where it still exists. Bentham was eventually compensated by Parliament with £23,000 for his efforts in working on the project for many years, but he never lost the bitterness he experienced from the rejection of his scheme and the many wasted years involved.

On imprisonment generally Bentham saw some disadvantages but thought it perfect in regard to disablement, eminently divisible in duration and very susceptible to different degrees of severity. Whilst prisoners were not seen, which did not help deter others, the prison itself was visible and might well strike terror. Indeed, he went on to suggest that prisons to hold medium, and long-term offenders should exhibit on the outside various figures such as a monkey, a fox and a tiger representing mischief, cunning, and rapacity. Inside should be placed two skeletons to represent the abode of death. In this, as on many other occasions Bentham was clearly impressed by the utility of visual aids.

The Rise of the Penitentiary

In 1816 a penitentiary was built at Millbank in place of the doomed Panopticon. The inmates were carefully chosen and were in the main young first offenders. A principal purpose was rehabilitation and prisoners were given separate cells, vocational employment and religious instruction. The normal practice in prisons of flogging those who offended against discipline was strictly forbidden. Prisoners received income for their work which was paid to them on their discharge with a gratuity of £3, to be doubled after a year, on proof of good conduct.

On the debit side the prison resembled a Gothic fortress with damp underground punishment cells. The staff were corrupt and violent and the food, consisting of bread, gruel and thin soup, was inadequate. There were constant troubles and when the Medical Superintendent put these down to over-eating the diet was cut. As a consequence typhus and scurvy broke out and after 31 inmates had died the remaining 400 were either released or transferred to the Hulks. Subsequently re-opened, trouble re-surfaced and in 1844 the Millbank was closed as a failure.

In the meantime the humanitarian appeal of both utilitarianism and evangelicalism was having some success in improving hygiene and discipline in local prisons. A long overdue classification of prisoners according to their sex and their offence was also introduced. At the same time crime and poverty were increasing and both were generating extreme prison overcrowding. Social control was always seen by Bentham as a major purpose of penal law and most Whig prison reformers agreed with him. The perceived need then for a reformative regime, combined with strict discipline following the Millbank disaster, led to separate confinement and Pentonville.[22]

Pentonville was opened in 1842 with solitary

---

22.   For a full and interesting treatment of Pentonville and its context *cf.* Michael Ignatieff. *A Just Measure of Pain.* 1978.

confinement, hard labour, which included the treadwheel and stone breaking, and religious instruction as its declared means to rehabilitation. It was intended to be a model for all new penitentiaries as well as for local prisons. It also reflected the social discipline of the extending factory environment outside. The strains of industrialization, including increased criminality, were considered to require more stringent modes of social control. In other words a more authoritarian type of state and employer for the supervision and discipline of the lower classes of society. After all, James Watt, Josiah Wedgwood, Abraham Darby and others not only financed reform causes, they were also the fathers of a factory system which introduced new means of labour discipline.[23]

Each prisoner was to spend 18 months in solitude in his cell, in contrast to the silent association system, before being sent to the public works prisons at Portland, Chatham and Dartmoor or being transported. Even the daily exercise period was spent alone in a small yard. Prisoners were often masked in order that they could not see one another or communicate, and there were separate stalls in chapel to prevent even the slightest conversation. Work in the cells usually involved working on prison boots and clothing. The regime was extremely punitive and there were many suicides and a great deal of mental derangement. As late as 1877 the suicide rate in English prisons was 17.6 per 1,000.

Prior to the abandonment of transportation which had taken care of long-term convicts, prison sentences were often short with a normal maximum of three years. With the decline and then demise of transportation in the middle of the century, sentences of 10 years' imprisonment became normal. Fifty-four new prisons

---

23.   *Cf.* Ignatieff. *Ibid.* 62.

were built on the model of Pentonville, providing 11,000 separate cells.[24] By 1856, returns made to Parliament showed about one third of the prisons in England employing the separate system exclusively and another third partially. Presumably the remainder had insufficient cell accommodation to do so.

The stated purpose of the whole "Pentonville policy", and in particular the cruel separation system, was to improve the prisoners' minds with a view to reformation. This was to be achieved by a combination of hard labour, instruction from the chaplain and an opportunity in the cells to reflect and repent of their crimes. It bears comparison with the twentieth century Chinese "brainwashing" technique used on prisoners of war in the Korean War, although it was perhaps less successful.

The serious effects of this repressive regime on the prisoners' bodies and minds caused considerable public disquiet, reflected by Dickens in *David Copperfield*.[25] The consequence was that in 1850, under Sir Joshua Jebb, Pentonville ceased to be a penitentiary and became instead a convict prison. An association exercise yard was provided, the partitions in the chapel were removed and the original 18 months' preliminary confinement was reduced first to one year and later to nine months.

An Act of 1853 then introduced penal servitude as a replacement for the declining punishment of transportation. Four years' penal servitude was set as the equivalent of the minimum sentence for transportation of seven years. The punishment involved hard labour on public works and was intended to act as a deterrent, both to the convict himself and to potential criminals. The statute also provided that for good behaviour a convict could be granted a ticket-of-leave which enabled him to

---

24.   Lionel W. Fox. *op. cit.* 38.
25.   Chapter 61. 779. *Folio Socy.* 1983. edn.

live outside the prison for the remainder of his term provided he behaved himself. This provoked widespread fear among the public but led eventually to the modern parole system.

Where, as in Ipswich, sufficiently arduous hard labour was not available, the treadwheel, or "everlasting staircase", was introduced into local prisons by the magistrates. This was invented around 1818, after earlier, more primitive types, by Samuel Cubitt, a native of Ipswich whose name is now known world-wide. Intended for his local JPs, the idea had been enthusiastically adopted by other justices throughout the country by 1824. It was also highly praised by Sydney Smith. It comprised a huge revolving wheel with steps which the prisoners continuously mounted to make it turn.

Six, 12 or 18 prisoners would step side by side from morning to night, treading some 8,640 feet in distance to grind corn or raise water or even simply air, until they were half killed.[26] People with bad legs, pregnant women and men with hernias joined other prisoners indiscriminately as a consequence of the general intoxication of the magistrates for the machine. As this "wholesome influence", as the prison inspector called it, continued to maim and kill, it also put additional power into the hands of the warders who could tighten the spring to make it unbearably painful. Incredible as it may seem, hard labour was not abolished until the Criminal Justice Act of 1948.

Alongside the government-run convict prisons the local gaols, still overseen by the magistrates, had continued to fester. In the main they held debtors, minor offenders and some convicts awaiting transportation. By the Prisons Act 1877 they were all nationalized and brought under government control with the appointment of a Prison

---

26.   S. & B. Webb. *English Prisons under Local Government.* 98. 1922.

Commission under the chairmanship of Sir Edmund Du Cane.

In convict prisons a prisoner now underwent nine months' separate confinement in his cell. He was then sent to a public works prison such as Dartmoor, with association at work but no talking, for three quarters of the remainder of his sentence with release on licence for the remaining quarter. The Act introduced a common standard with longer sentences, less nourishing food and stricter discipline. However, Du Cane's enthusiastic enforcement of the new regime led to near-disaster and public outrage. Changes in the philosophy and practice of imprisonment as a punishment became inevitable and these will be discussed in ch.11 on the twentieth century - a century of improvement.

Garrotting

Crimes of violence were on the increase in the 1850s and panic set in when an outbreak of garrotting occurred in various parts of the country in 1862. Garrotting involved choking, suffocating or strangling a victim in the course of committing an indictable offence. In response to the public panic the Judges immediately began to order floggings in addition to penal servitude in an endeavour to stem the growing disorder that the crime was causing. Their example was soon followed by Parliament which, against the wishes of the government, enacted the Security from Violence Act 1863.

This permitted Judges to order flogging once, twice or thrice in addition to imprisonment or penal servitude. For offenders over the age of 16 this could mean 150 lashes and for those under 16, 75 lashes. Ironically in the event, the epidemic of garrotting died out before the Act became law. Although the Judges claimed the credit of its demise for flogging, it is more likely that penal servitude for life was the true deterrent.

Deodands

These "hallowed mysteries"[27] from the past seemed to have faded by the eighteenth century. In the early nineteenth century, however, they enjoyed a revival as a means of providing compensation for accidents caused by factory machines and death-dealing railway engines. In Hale's day only the offending wheel of a cart which caused death could be forfeit, but by nineteenth century judgments of the courts a whole railway carriage and a coach and horses could be taken. For example, in 1838 the railway engines *Merlin* and *Basilish* collided and both were forfeited. This change ensured a more substantial payment of compensation to widows who had no right of action for economic loss on the death of a breadwinner following a harsh ruling in the case of *Baker* v. *Bolton* in 1808.

Railway companies in particular suffered heavy deodand awards against them, at times up to £2,000, but in 1846 Lord Campbell introduced a Fatal Accidents' Bill to help widows of men killed in accidents caused by the act of another. At the same time he introduced a second Bill, this to abolish deodands. Both travelled together throughout their successful passage through Parliament, even though Campbell complained that 80 members of the Commons could be mustered by one railway company alone to vote against the first Bill.

Thus did deodands disappear from English legal history, although it is sad to record that the Fatal

---

27.   Harry Smith. "From Deodand to Dependency." *American Journal of Legal History*. vol.11. 389. (1967).

Accidents Act dismally failed to provide adequate compensation in most cases brought under it as a consequence of its interpretation by the Judges. Indeed many relatives of victims of railway accidents were left with no rights of compensation at all against the railway companies who could often rely upon the defences of common employment and contributory negligence which had been no answer to deodands. It seems curious that Campbell thought the latter were hostile to a Bill which was so advantageous to them.

Deodands also had an interesting parallel in the so-called penal compensation which, under the early Factories and Mines Acts, magistrates could award to the victims of industrial accidents or their families. Following Bentham's concept of criminal compensation, these statutes enabled the whole, or part, of a fine inflicted for a breach of their provisions to be applied as civil compensation in criminal proceedings. Local benches of magistrates frequently proved hostile to the scheme, but the concept was not abandoned until the Factories Act 1959. Today, of course, magistrates and Judges may order an offender to pay compensation for any personal injury, loss or damage arising from his offence.

Whipping

Corporal punishment continued to be acceptable in English public life throughout the nineteenth century. It is true that whipping was withdrawn from public gaze as a deterrent in 1817 but it continued to flourish, particularly in prisons, houses of correction, the armed forces, and for juveniles. Most prisons possessed a "cat-o'-nine-tails" for use on erring convicts who were strapped to a large triangle with feet and arms asunder as I witnessed in a British gaol in Aden in 1962. Such floggings were agonizingly painful and a sickening and demeaning spectacle.

For violently resisting a constable a "rogue and vagabond" could be sent to prison and undergo whipping. This, said Peel, was "a salutary terror, which checked the growth of such offences."[28] Juveniles could be whipped instead of, or in addition to, going to prison. By the Whipping of Offenders Act of 1862, however, the number of strokes of the birch was restricted to 12, no person was to be whipped more than once for the same offence and whippings were henceforth to be in private. As we have seen these safeguards were abandoned within a year for the crime of garrotting, but that was a panic measure. However, only with the Criminal Justice Act of 1948 was the whipping of young children forbidden.

Floggings in the army and navy were also a regular occurrence with up to 200 lashes with a "cat-o-nine-tails." On June 15, 1846 Frederick John White, a private of the Seventh Hussars, received a severe and cruel flogging of 150 lashes at the Cavalry Barracks on Hounslow Heath after an enforced 17 hours fast. Several soldiers who witnessed the flogging fainted on the spot. White was even refused a drink of tea whilst in agony after the flogging. Unfortunately for the government this was within the jurisdiction as Coroner of Dr. Thomas Wakley, MP. White died on July 11. Without really examining his back three army doctors declared that the flogging had nothing to do with his death, and this was repeated by government spokesmen in the House of Commons.

Wakley, however, attended the scene and summoned an inquest jury. He also called in a specialist, Erasmus Wilson of the Middlesex Hospital, who, after examining the lacerated body, had no difficulty in convincing the jury that death was caused by the flogging. The jury had also

---

28.   *Hansard.* (June 3, 1824). vol.11, col.1085.

seen the body and in giving their verdict expressed their "horror and disgust" at the law which permitted the "revolting punishment of flogging to be inflicted upon British soldiers." They implored every man in the kingdom to join "hand and heart" in forwarding petitions to the legislature praying for the abolition of such a disgraceful practice, which was a "slur upon the humanity and fair name of the people of this country." Serious public concern was instantly aroused. As a consequence the case was debated in Parliament and flogging in the army largely fell into disuse until it was finally abolished by the Army Act of 1881.

Until corporal punishment was abolished in 1948 it continued in use in civilian life with a good deal of public approval, strong remnants of which still exist today. Stephen, however, expressed clearly the contrary view when he wrote, "no punishment varies so much in amount, none affords such scope for tyranny, for bad temper, or for malignity and cruelty. It is moreover irremissible when once inflicted; and it is usually too short to admit of much permanent influence being brought to bear on the person who suffers it."[29] An argument not only somewhat contradictory in itself but also a curious contrast to his views on analogy noted earlier.

We should not conclude this review of punishments in the nineteenth century without paying tribute to the reformers who understood what was new in their own day and assisted in making it a century of criminal and penal law reform. In consequence of the unremitting efforts of Romilly, Bentham, Peel, Brougham, Russell and many others, death ceased to be the principal punishment available to, and staining, the criminal law. Prisoners were permitted counsel on their trial for felony from 1836.

---

29.   "Essays by a Barrister." *The Saturday Review.* 147. (1862).

Juvenile offenders received more speedy trial and less severe punishment, and the incompetency of witnesses was removed in 1843. The period between sentence and the execution of a convicted murderer was increased and many innocent prisoners were reprieved as a result. Criminal procedure was also improved and many of the harsh penalties and disabilities for beliefs of religion and conscience were removed.

The pillory was abolished, as was forfeiture for high treason and felony. A new lesser offence of treason was introduced with treason-felony in 1848. Judges were also given power by Lord Denman's Act of 1846 to vary punishments in some instances to prevent injustices. A case in point, although not prevented by the Act, was recorded in *The Times* on February 4, 1847. At the Old Bailey one accused was found guilty of stealing a letter containing 10 shillings. He was transported for 10 years. At the same court, on the same day, another accused was found to have terminated a long course of brutality towards his own wife by kicking her to death. He was let off with nine months' hard labour. According to the newspaper such a striking instance of the disparity between crimes and punishments was to be seen at most sittings of the Old Bailey.

Bearing in mind the full horror of the penal law when the nineteenth century dawned, perhaps we can endorse the view of Andrew Amos, one of the 1834 Criminal Law Commissioners, who described the statutes referred to above in his *Ruins of Time exemplified in Sir Matthew Hale's Pleas of the Crown* in 1856 as the "noblest trophies of our age in the cause of Criminal Law Reform."[30]

---

30.   *Preface.* xvi.

CHAPTER 10

CRIMINAL INCAPACITY

Liability

It might seem at first glance that the topic of incapacity has no place in a book on punishment. However, the essence of the subject is whether or not to punish at all and, if so, how? In that sense it is relevant. With the exception of offences of strict liability, all allegations of crime are subject to specific defences such as alibi or the absence of intention. Of course, proving them is by no means always easy, indeed they frequently raise serious problems. Yet even more complex are the general defences based on incapacity. If permitted at all, these apply to all cases including those of strict responsibility and, if successful, they secure exemption from all punishment.

From a utilitarian point of view punishing offenders who have no ability to know they are doing wrong is unjust, since it can have no deterrent effect either on the actor himself or those similarly placed. Nevertheless, English law has always been slow to accept such factors as insanity, intoxication, compulsion and necessity as sufficient defences to the commission of crimes. No doubt the possibility of fabrication is an important element contributing to this reluctance, and it has often been considered that incapacity should merely go to the mitigation of punishment.

Sir Matthew Hale devoted eight chapters of his *History of the Pleas of the Crown*[1] to dealing with incapacity as a possible defence in capital cases, although in a rather rudimentary fashion. Let us consider the history of a few of these topics.

Infancy

At the time of writing a number of Judges have deplored the fact that they are prevented by law from dealing adequately with some persistent and vicious young criminals because of their age. The facts of some of the cases involving multiple thefts, rape and other offences of violence make shocking reading.

In Hale's time a young person over the age of 14 was considered capable of discerning between good and evil and was subject to capital punishment. Between the ages of seven and 14 very strong evidence of that ability was required before the jury could convict but Hale mentioned cases where infants of eight, 10 and 13 had been executed. Infants under seven could not be tried at all as there was a legal presumption that they were incapable of discerning between good and evil.

Today no child under the age of 10 years can be found guilty of an offence. The presumption that he or she is not capable of crime is irrebuttable. But the common law rule that between the ages of 10 and 14 a child had to be proved to know right from wrong has been overturned by the Court of Appeal in *C (a minor)* v. *DPP* (1994). An under-14 child can only be detained in custody for serious offences, and for young persons aged 14 and over, only if the offence has a normal maximum penalty of 14 years

---

1.   Chapters 2-9.

or more. However, a new Criminal Justice Bill proposes to introduce a secure training order. This will be a new punishment to be given to juveniles aged 12-14 who have committed at least three separate offences. They can then be sent to a secure training unit for a maximum of one year.

At the time of writing a boy of 14 with 43 convictions of serious crimes has been returned to the care of the local authority from whom he has previously escaped 25 times. The court has no power to send him to secure accommodation. Before the passing of the Sexual Offences Act, 1993 at common law boys under 14 were also presumed incapable of sexual intercourse and thus could not be convicted of rape, which was an example of the law making an ass of itself. A more detailed examination of the punishment, as distinct from the incapacity, of young persons will be made in the next chapter.

Madness

By the law of England, wrote Hale, generally no man could avoid the consequences of his own act by pleading madness. He was the first jurist, however, to distinguish between total and partial insanity. This, he thought, would enable the Judge and jury to draw a line between an inhuman approach to the defects of human nature and too great an indulgence to serious crimes. According to Professor Nigel Walker, Hale's exposition was "... to exercise the minds of lawyers, psychiatrists and Royal Commissions for the next three centuries."[2]

Defences of insanity were sometimes successful in the seventeenth century. But the two following centuries saw a change with a series of convictions in important trials

---

2.   *Crime and Insanity in England.* 38. 1968.

after a number of murders of, and attempts on the lives of, royalty, prime ministers and nobles. Some of these were to be discussed by the Judges in attempting to set out a clear position following the *M'Naghten* case in March 1843.

The *M'Naghten* Rules

Daniel M'Naghten claimed that "the Tories" were trying to kill him and in response he fatally shot Peel's private secretary in mistake for Peel. M'Naghten's defence was that partial insanity was within the law of insanity and that he was partially insane - it being impossible on the evidence to prove full insanity.

His counsel, Alexander Cockburn QC, (later Lord Chief Justice), argued that M'Naghten's insanity consisted of a delusion directed to one or more persons which took away all power of self-control. His brilliant conduct of the defence secured from the jury an acquittal which shocked the public. One MP even sought leave to introduce a Bill to abolish completely any plea of insanity in cases of murder or attempted murder. Parliament refused to be panicked, however, and the House of Lords proceeded to debate the issue in what Brougham called the "present emergency".

Lord Chancellor Lyndhurst and others asserted that despite the M'Naghten verdict there was no serious defect in the law on insanity. In a letter to Peel,[3] Lyndhurst wrote that the law of monomania had been correctly laid down in the case of Bowler[4] who was tried in 1812 for firing a loaded blunderbuss at a William Burrows and

---

3.   *BM. Add. Mss.* 40442. Peel Correspondence with Lyndhurst. fol.138. 1841-49.

4.   O.B.S.P. case 527. (1812).

wounding him. The Judge had told the jury that it was for them to determine whether the prisoner, when he committed the offence, was under the influence of any illusion regarding the victim which made him at the moment insensible to the nature of the act he was about to commit. If he were, he would not be legally responsible for his conduct.

Lord Mansfield had said substantially the same in the case of Bellingham[5] who was sentenced to death for fatally shooting dead the Prime Minister, Spencer Perceval, in the lobby of the House of Commons. According to Stephen, Bellingham was arrested, committed, tried and hanged all within little more than a week in order to prevent him setting up the defence of madness.[6] In fact the murder was committed on May 11 and the trial and conviction took place at the Old Bailey on Saturday, May 16. Romilly, who considered Bellingham mad but a danger to mankind who should not be exempt from punishment, nevertheless thought the defence application to put back the trial to give him time to bring witnesses from Liverpool was "very reasonable."[7]

Another trial of interest was that of Hadfield who was charged with treason in 1800 having come within inches of killing George III in a box at Drury Lane Theatre. On the testimony of witnesses, his counsel, the celebrated Thomas Erskine, had little difficulty in establishing his client's insanity. But Hadfield was clearly aware of the nature of his act, as well as the fact that it was unlawful, since he had planned it carefully and its purpose was to ensure that he was executed for treason.

However, Erskine was able to circumvent the normal test of ability to distinguish right and wrong by arguing

---

5.   *Ibid.* case 433. (1812).
6.   *Cambridge Essays.* 38. 1859.
7.   *Memoirs. Op. cit.* iii. 36.

that Hadfield suffered from the delusion that he must be destroyed, but must not destroy himself. In fact, Hadfield's delusion was that the world was coming to an end and that he was commissioned by God to save mankind by the sacrifice of himself otherwise than by suicide.

The Judge, Lord Kenyon, accepted Erskine's argument and told the jury that if the scales hung anything like even, it was their duty to throw in "a certain proportion of mercy." They responded by acquitting Hadfield with the verdict, "not guilty on the ground of insanity." This wording continued in use until 1883 when Queen Victoria was shot at by a man subsequently acquitted as being insane. The Queen complained that he should have been found guilty, and by a statute of that year it was provided that the formula should be changed to "guilty of the act or omission charged against him, but insane at the time."[8] This, however, obscured the fact that in law the verdict was really one of acquittal from which no appeal was possible. Today the verdict has reverted to "not guilty by reason of insanity."

To return to the House of Lords debate on the *M'Naghten* case, most of their Lordships agreed with the Lord Chancellor that the existing law was satisfactory but, in order to placate public opinion, they agreed to summon the Judges to give their opinion of the law. The House took the unusual step of submitting a number of questions to the Judges whose replies, known to subsequent generations as the *M'Naghten* Rules, became law.

From that time onwards it was a defence to show defect of reason due to disease of the mind based on either not knowing the nature and quality of the act (eg, automatism or mistake of fact), or if these were known,

---

8.   *Trial of Lunatics Act*, s.2(1).

not knowing they were wrong. This was not to mean, as before, morally wrong, but wrong according to the law of the land. However, it was not until 1952, in the case of *Windle*,[9] that the Court of Criminal Appeal finally confirmed this to be the test for the jury.

If insanity were limited to a delusion, an accused would be free of punishment only if the delusion would have justified his act in law if it were true. On this basis M'Naghten would have been convicted and since that time Judges have proceeded on the assumption that a deluded man can be presumed to be normal in all other respects, unless there is evidence to the contrary. And whereas today many psychiatrists and clinical psychologists see most mental disorders in terms of differences of degree, the criminal law still expects diagnoses to fit a verdict of guilty or not guilty.

However, by s.2 of the Homicide Act of 1957, although irresistible impulse and mental disorder falling short of insanity are generally no defence on a charge of murder, a verdict of manslaughter must be returned if the accused is found to be suffering from diminished responsibility. This allows the Judge a discretion as to punishment which is not available in cases of murder.

Intoxication

In Coke's time drunkenness could never be a defence unless induced by unskilled medical treatment or the action of a man's enemies. We have already noted the proverb, "he that kyllyth a man dronk, sobur schal be hangyd." Hale, however, wanted to see the rule modified for an habitual drunkard who caused himself a permanently diseased intellect. He discussed the

---

9.   2 Q.B. 826 (C.C.A.).

difficulties of proving the dementia of drunkenness but largely relied upon the jury to resolve the problems.

By the nineteenth century the rigidity of the old rule had been gradually relaxed by judicial decisions. For his part Bentham thought that "perfect intoxication", like insanity, should exempt an offender from punishment on the utilitarian ground that it could not deter the offender from repeating his offence. He considered the existing law to be hard and unthinking, but he saw the dangers and added that anyone who knew by experience that wine rendered him dangerous deserved no indulgence for those excesses into which it might lead him.[10]

In 1819, in the case of *R. v. Grindley*,[11] temporary insanity was held to excuse murder where the killing was on a "sudden heat and impulse" caused by drunkenness. This doctrine was overruled by *R. v. Carroll*[12] in 1835, when it was pleaded as a defence by a soldier who, when drunk, had stabbed a man with his bayonet. Park J., in his judgment, declared of the doctrine that "there would be no safety for human life if it were to be considered as law." His view was modified in three subsequent cases and in *R. v. Cruse* in 1838, where a drunken man knocked a child's head against a beam, it was left to the jury to decide whether the prisoner had a murderous intent at the time of the attack and he was acquitted of murder. In fact, statute[13] made intent to murder essential to the crime.

Generally speaking, today drunkenness remains no excuse for crime, except where it is involuntary or where it results in permanent or temporary insanity.[14] But it

---

10. *Principles of Morals and Legislation.* 79.
11. *Russel on Crimes.* 8. (2nd edn.).
12. 7 C. & P. 145.
13. 1 Vict. c.85, s.2.
14. *Cf. R. v. Kingston* (1993) and the reliance of the Court of Appeal on Hale's "classic statement of principle" on drunkenness as a defence.

is of importance if it can be proved to negate a mental element essential to the charge. This particularly applies to crimes such as murder and theft where it may negate specific intent, recklessness or specific knowledge. The evidential burden is now on the prosecution to establish that, despite the evidence of intoxication, the accused had the necessary specific intent. However, recent cases show that the problems are still far from being resolved. A serious attempt to deal with them is made in the 1985 Report to the Law Commission on *Codification of the Criminal Law.*[15]

Necessity

This defence involves an assertion that certain conduct promotes a higher value than a literal compliance with the law. An example might be pulling down a house to prevent a fire from spreading. The concept has a long history and Bracton declared that what was not otherwise lawful was made so by necessity.[16] As long ago as 1499 Rede J. said that jurors might lawfully depart from the court without leave of the Judge if an affray broke out and they were in peril of death, or if the courtroom fell down.[17] A good deal later, in 1815, the Judges held that although it was a misdemeanour to expose an infected person in public, necessity would be a defence to the charge if, for example, a sick child was carried through the streets to a doctor.[18]

Such cases led Stephen to say that the law on the defence of necessity was vague and that the Judges could

---

15. *Law Com.* 143. paras.9.7-9.22. See also *Law Com.* 177 and 208.
16. Quoted by Coke. *2 Inst.* 362.
17. Y.B.T. 14 Hen.7, 196, pl.4.
18. *Vantandillo.* 4 M. & S. 73 (1815).

lay down any rule they thought expedient.[19] The law had been modified, he thought, since Hale had held that killing an innocent person could never be justified. Blackstone was of the opinion that Hale's view should stand but be softened if necessary by the prerogative of mercy.

In the well-known case of *R. v. Dudley and Stephens*[20] in 1884 Coleridge C.J. indicated both the difficulties and the danger of framing a general defence of necessity. In that case shipwrecked sailors killed their cabin boy for food. The jury found that if the men had not fed upon the body of the boy they would probably not have survived to be picked up and rescued, and that the boy, being in a much weaker condition, would have died before them. Nevertheless, the sailors were found guilty of murder and sentenced to death although, adopting Blackstone's view, the Crown reduced the sentence to one of six months' imprisonment.

So difficult is it to define a defence of necessity that even a recent Law Commission Report omitted it from a draft Criminal Code Bill, except for action immediately necessary to avoid death or serious injury, and declared that it should remain a matter of common law.[21]

It was long held that where duress induced a well-grounded fear of death or grievous bodily harm it should excuse a person from punishment, except in cases of treason and homicide. In the latter case Blackstone followed Hale in thinking that a man should rather die himself than escape by the murder of an innocent.[22] However, in the leading case of *Tyler* and *Price*[23] in 1838 Lord Denman held that duress could be no defence to any

---

19.   *Op. cit.* ii. 108.
20.   14 Q.B.D. 273 (1884).
21.   *Law Com.* 143. 120. (1985).
22.   *Op. cit.* 30.
23.   8 C. & P. 616.

illegal act. Today, on the contrary, duress is a defence in itself since the harm sought to be avoided proceeds from another's wrongdoing, unlike necessity where it may arise from an infinite variety of circumstances. The test is whether in all the circumstances the conduct of the accused can be excused.

The defence is not applicable to murder, however, since the House of Lords decision in the case of *Howe* in 1987. Among the reasons given by their lordships, in line with the views of Hale and Blackstone, is that the protection of the life of an innocent person is of supreme importance and that a person should be required to sacrifice his own life rather than be permitted to decide who should live and who should die.

It is an interesting fact that, in regard to duress and the other defences of incapacity, legislation is not very prolific and the complexities of this aspect of the law are still left to the courts to resolve, if they can. In this connexion the views and proposals contained in the *Report on Codification of the Criminal Law* submitted by the Law Commission to Parliament in 1985 and the Commission's own Criminal Code[24] are significant, although too detailed to be considered here.

---

24.   *Op. cit.*

CHAPTER 11

A CENTURY OF IMPROVEMENT

The Gladstone Report

By the end of the nineteenth century such faith as there had been in the prison system had evaporated. Contrary to expectations, recidivism was growing and separate confinement and the rule of silence were seen to be too harsh and cruel. In 1890 one observer, echoing Oliver Goldsmith over a century earlier, wrote that the English prison system was, "a manufactory of lunatics and criminals."[1] As usual there were wide differences of opinion between those responsible for the prison service as to who was to blame and what should be done. Prison Commissioner Sir Edmund Du Cane was severely criticized for the failure of the system by those who perceived a new policy of reformation and rehabilitation of individual prisoners to be the solution.

Widespread public disquiet led the government to appoint what became a famous departmental committee on prisons under the chairmanship of Mr Herbert Gladstone. *The Gladstone Report on Prisons* was published in 1895[2] and set forth the twin themes of "deterrence and reform" by means of training and

---

1.   A.W. Renton. 6 *LQR*. 338.
2.   C. 2nd series, 7703. LV1.

treatment. These goals were to set the tone for twentieth century attempts at penal reform alongside improving life in the prisons.

Among other measures, the Report recommended the abolition of the treadwheel, less solitary confinement and a better diet. This was backed by a strong feeling that it was desirable to keep as many offenders as possible out of prison altogether. Recidivism, the Report declared, was "a growing stain on our civilization." And, overturning a century of penal philosophy, it recognized that separate confinement led to moral and mental deterioration and that the silence rule was unnatural.

As a result, the dawn of the twentieth century saw a spate of improving statutes. These were directed at giving effect to the new thinking which was part of the political change taking place in the country. The turn of the century was witnessing a decline in the economic fortunes of Britain, the birth of the welfare state, the formation of the labour party, the successes of the liberal party and widespread industrial unrest.

The forerunner of the statutes was the Prison Act of 1898 which reduced the number of offences for which flogging could be inflicted, established a system for classifying offenders and introduced remission for good conduct. Three other statutes were soon enacted to give effect to the desire to avoid giving some offenders the stigma of imprisonment. The first, in 1907, was the Probation of Offenders Act which empowered the courts to suspend a sentence on condition the offender was placed under the supervision of a probation officer.

Then, in 1908, Parliament passed the Children Act which forbade the imprisonment of children under 14 years of age. It also provided that those between 14 and 16 could only be sent to prison if the court granted a special certificate stating that they were unruly and depraved. As a consequence, whereas 572 youths of under

16 were sent to prison in 1907, the number was reduced to 18 by 1925.[3]

The year 1908 also saw the Prevention of Crime Act which ensured that young offenders aged 16-21 who were liable to imprisonment should be sent to Borstals instead. Sentences were indeterminate, and often longer than they would otherwise have been since here the youngsters were to receive between two and three years of training followed by a year under supervision. Despite all the odds against it, Borstal treatment as it developed was considered to be a success, until the experienced and caring staff (and many of the inmates) were required for other duties in World War II.

Another, and more controversial, provision of the Act for indeterminate sentences was that for "habitual criminals" who could be sentenced to penal servitude and an added period of preventive detention for up to 10 years. When Winston Churchill became Home Secretary in 1910 he expressed deep concern about the possible effects of this provision.

"I have serious misgivings," he said, "lest the institution of preventive detention should lead to a reversion to the ferocious sentences of the last generation. After all preventive detention is penal servitude in all essentials, but it soothes the conscience of Judges and of public and there is a very grave danger that the administration of the law should under softer names assume in fact a more severe character."[4]

Unfortunately, Churchill's forebodings proved justified and many cases of injustice resulted. Some of them

---

3.   *Report of Committee on Treatment of Young Offenders.* Cmd. 2381. 12. 1927.

4.   *HO.* 144/1002/134165.

Churchill was able to mitigate until his view prevailed and preventive detention sentences were gradually phased out. He also used his position at the Home Office to visit prisons and call for improvements in conditions. In one case he ordered the immediate release of a number of incarcerated juveniles whom he met.

In the years leading up to the Second World War, the effects of the legislation inspired by Gladstone were tested. So far as prison conditions are concerned they were revealed still to be appalling in 1919 from the first-hand experiences of them related by Hobhouse and Brockway in *English Prisons Today*. Despite the improvements mentioned above convicts continued to have their hair cropped, still wore clothes covered with broad arrows and still spent as many as 17 out of 24 hours in their cells. They were humiliated, treated like caged animals and suffered from degrading and filthy sanitary arrangements.

Many of these horrors were to be remedied by the prison reforms of the humanitarian Sir Alexander Paterson while he was a prison commissioner between 1922 and 1947. It was Paterson who coined the phrase, "men come to prison as a punishment not *for* punishment" and that summed up his underlying philosophy which did so much to alleviate the deplorable lot of prisoners at that time.

Apart from prison conditions there was little call for penal reform in the inter-war years, although useful research was undertaken which would have led to some new measures had the Second World War not intervened.

One example was the work of the Cadogan Committee on corporal punishment in 1938.[5] This committee analysed the records of 440 prisoners convicted of robbery with violence between the years 1921 and 1930. It

---

5.   *H.O.* Cmd. 5684.

compared the subsequent careers of those who had been flogged as a punishment with those who had not. Those flogged were found to have the worse records of further crime. The Report is a reminder that in 1938 the birch and the cat-o'-nine-tails were still in use although with a maximum of 36 strokes. Reform was delayed by the war, however, and whipping as a punishment was not finally abolished until the Criminal Justice Act 1948, although even then it was retained for grave assaults on prison officers and mutiny in prison.

Post-war Reform

The 1948 Act introduced corrective training and provided for another attempt at preventive detention, this time of a fixed term of between five and 14 years for a person aged 30 or over whose present crime was serious and who had a number of previous convictions. This, the Act said, was for the protection of society (repeating the argument of the 1908 Act) although the Cadogan Committee in 1938 had questioned whether it was ethically sound to make an example of one person for the benefit of the community. More importantly the Act abolished both penal servitude and hard labour and replaced them with ordinary imprisonment.

Some 20 years later the Criminal Justice Act of 1967 abolished both corrective training and preventive detention - the special punishments for persistent offenders which punished them for previous offences already punished. In their place it introduced the extended sentence. This empowered a court to extend a sentence beyond the normal length (or even, in limited circumstances, beyond the statutory maximum), where the offender's record justified a term to protect the public. This provision has, however, been little used. The Act further nullified the ancient distinction between felony and misdemeanour which had caused so much injustice in the past.

One of the major changes introduced by the Act, against the advice of the advisory council on the treatment of offenders, was to empower the courts to suspend a sentence. As a consequence a sentence pronounced but suspended is only activated or modified if a further offence is committed during the period of the suspension. This was one of several measures introduced in this period to avoid imprisonment where possible. Others included partial suspension of a sentence, attendance centre orders and community service orders.

We might also mention Grendon Underwood in Buckinghamshire which was opened in 1962 as a psychiatric prison. Inmates there are serious offenders who, with their consent or at their own request, have been transferred from other prisons. If found unsuitable or endeavouring to escape they are removed. The staff to prisoner ratio is one to one, with the staff including psychiatrists. Groups of prisoners meet every day as a therapy with a psychiatrist present. There is association, work and no overcrowding. The aims are to help the prisoners overcome their disorders and to obtain knowledge about such disorders and how to treat them. The conclusions drawn by the Home Office from this experiment may prove to be valuable but there seems little likelihood of the experiment being extended if only because the cost of the staff prisoner ratio would prove prohibitive.

Turning for a moment to a different jurisdiction it is also interesting that in the 1960s the State of California built a number of new commodious prisons to house all its prisoners for indeterminate periods. The theory of the time was that since prisons could reform criminals the inmates should remain there until they were "cured" of their criminality. In other words, the punishment was not to fit the crime but was to be determined by the performance of the offender in prison. Naturally prison staff assumed an important role in the ensuing decisions of parole boards. Not surprisingly awful anomalies resulted. Men sentenced for the same crime suffered vastly different periods of confinement and some endured up to 25 years incarceration for minor offences. Needless to say the system did not survive.

Returning to England, so far as children and young persons are concerned we have already looked at the background of the age of responsibility in ch.10. But the law has come a long way in the last 150 years. In 1849, for example, 10,703 young persons under 17 years of age were transported whilst prisons held a similar number.

Today we have police cautions to avoid bringing some young people before the courts at all. Youth courts have now replaced juvenile courts but have retained all their powers - discharges, binding over, fines, compensation orders, attendance centre orders and supervision orders. For 16- and 17-year-olds there are also probation, community service and combination orders; with detention in a young offenders' institution an alternative for 15 - 17-year-olds. A custodial sentence can be passed on a young offender now only if he or she has a history of failure to respond to non-custodial penalties; or only a custodial sentence is adequate to protect the public from serious harm; or the offence is so serious that a non-custodial sentence cannot be justified.

Where bail is refused to young people, remands are made into local authority accommodation but the courts now have authority, under the Criminal Justice Act 1991, to impose conditions previously denied to them, such as a curfew, restrictions of activities and restrictions on contact with named individuals. Considerable doubt has been expressed, however, as to how successful these new powers will be in preventing young offenders breaking such conditions, or absconding and committing further crimes, since the consequence of doing so are minimal. In response, the Home Secretary has indicated that some persistent young offenders will be sent to secure detention centres.

The Act's limitation on sentencing extends also to adults. This is in part a response to the fact that before the Act this country was imprisoning more people per hundred thousand than any other country in Western Europe. Now a custodial sentence is available for adults only if the offence is so serious that only imprisonment is justified. In the case of a sexual or violent offence, however, prison can also be invoked if the court considers it necessary to protect the public from serious harm, or the offender refuses to consent to a community sentence. However, after widespread public criticism, the Home Secretary announced in May 1993 that the size of the prison population "should be driven by the decision of the courts to send people to prison."

Furthermore, following the 1991 Act, the maximum sentences for certain offences were reduced. For example, the maximum sentence for theft was reduced from 10 years to seven years and that for burglary of commercial premises from 14 years to 10 years. Such reductions were the consequence of the Act increasing the earliest release date for prisoners from a minimum of one-third to one-half of the sentence. However, the maximum penalty for causing death by dangerous driving, or careless driving whilst under the influence of drink or drugs, has been increased from five to 10 years. For juveniles the offence is classifiable as a "grave crime" and punishable accordingly.

Under the Act, previous convictions were no longer to be taken into account in most cases on the ground that, like preventive detention, to do so punishes for offences already punished. The Act said "an offence shall not be regarded as more serious by reason of any previous conviction of the offender, or by reason of any failure of his to respond to previous sentences." This provision, and some bizarre consequences of it, met with much judicial criticism, however, and was amended by the Criminal Justice (Amendment) Act, 1993. This allows the court to take into account any previous convictions or failure to respond to previous sentences when considering seriousness. Also abolished were the Act's "unit fines" by which, for example, a drunken driver could be fined £212 and his passenger four times as much. The fixing of fines is now based upon the seriousness of the offence and the means of the offender.

Abolition of Hanging for Murder

After a life of more than a thousand years the demise of the death penalty must be applauded. After capital punishment had been restricted in practice to the crimes of murder and treason in the mid-nineteenth century, advocates of total abolition received scant support during the succeeding hundred years. Indeed, John Stuart Mill was highly praised for his presentation of the case for retention and when William Ewart died in 1867 the abolitionists were left without a charismatic leader.

In the twentieth century, Sir Alexander Paterson agreed with Mill that death was more humane than 20 years' imprisonment, which would often "permanently impair something more precious than the life of the physical body."[6] Only if life imprisonment were reduced to 10 years as an alternative to capital punishment would he accept abolition. A select committee of 1930, to which

---

6.   S.K. Ruck. *Paterson on Prisons.* 143.

Paterson gave evidence, recommended abolition for an experimental period of five years. This was not acceptable to the government of the day. However, a clause giving effect to this proposal appeared in the Criminal Justice Bill of 1948, only to be rejected by the House of Lords including many of its Judges.

The Home Secretary, Chuter Ede, then announced the setting up of a Royal Commission to study the *possible limitation* of the death penalty. Despite its narrow terms of reference, however, the Commission wisely considered that there was only a fine distinction between the evidence it took in relation to restriction and abolition. This was the issue, declared its Report, published in 1953.[7] Three controversial cases then emerged, including that of Timothy Evans who was wrongly found guilty of murdering his wife and his baby daughter, which made it clear that innocent men had lost their lives on the scaffold. As a consequence, before long the Homicide Bill of 1957 was welcomed in both Houses of Parliament. It became law and restricted the types of murder for which a person could be hanged to: those in the course of theft; by shooting or causing an explosion; the killing of a police officer or a prison officer acting in the execution of his duty; and second or subsequent murders.

Only a few years later, after a great deal of debate in Parliament the Murder (Abolition of the Death Penalty) Act 1965 succeeded in making the punishment for all murders imprisonment for life, with the Judge able to declare a minimum period. The last people to be hanged in Britain were Peter Allen and Gwynne Evans, in August 1964. The last woman to be executed was Ruth Ellis on July 13, 1955 at Holloway Prison. The only offences for which capital punishment now exists are treason, piracy and some under the Armed Forces Acts. Thus has finally

---

7.   *Cmd.* 8932.

ended the linchpin of the old law of felony whereby "hanging by the neck until dead" was the primary penalty for all serious crimes from the reign of Henry I.

A New Crime

The advent of motor vehicles in the twentieth century has brought a new dimension to the lives of most people. It has also seen introduced a plethora of Road Traffic Acts and Regulations. Normal penalties for breaches of the new laws are those familiar for other offences. But perhaps of most interest is the fixed penalty of a minimum disqualification from driving for those guilty of "drink-driving." For many motorists this sentence is an effective deterrent and it has undoubtedly saved many lives.

Added to which, police in the county of Sussex sometimes confiscate the driver's car in serious cases - a practice that may spread to the rest of the country. In any event the courts now have power to forfeit and sell a driver's car for exceptionally bad driving by virtue of the Road Traffic Act, 1991. This may be seen as a modern revival of our old friend the deodand and both the disqualification and the confiscation as new forms of social control since these punishments have serious consequences in an age of mass motoring, not least for the guilty driver's employment and the livelihood of himself and his family. Nevertheless the crime, for crime it is, has to be dealt with and discouraged vigorously.

Improvement

It cannot be denied that the system of punishments is now more flexible than at the commencement of the twentieth century. It is also more humane. Nevertheless, recipients of punishment now form a substantial minority of the population. Public interest in the question is high and, as one would expect, in a democracy there are many effective pressure groups and manifold influences on the government's decision-making processes.

The Home Office has its research teams, the police have their own means of expression, and MPs are not slow to express their views and those of their constituents. Magistrates, their clerks, probation officers, social service workers and prison officers all have specialist knowledge, based on direct experience of the criminal justice system, and their own proposals. The National Association for the Care and Resettlement of Offenders, the Howard League, civil liberties organizations and others also press what they regard as solutions to the problems.

This leads us to fundamental questions. Since no penal system has solved crime are punishments punitive acts of the state as part of its general strategy of rule and maintenance of that rule? And, if there is coercion, how far does it have to be modified or kept in a velvet glove (as Stephen thought) to retain legitimacy? Or, is the history of punishments a natural process of humanitarian reform produced by pressures in an ever-changing society? Such questions as these will be examined in the final chapter.

CHAPTER 12

THE POLITICS OF PUNISHMENT

Theories of Punishment

Like Bentham before him George Bernard Shaw considered that punishment injured and degraded the lawbreaker. Unlike Bentham he thought it could not also improve and reform him. In a Preface to the Webbs' *English Prisons under Local Government* in 1922 he declared that deterrence is a form of terrorism and that retribution and reformation are irreconcilable. For Shaw, only vengeance is achieved by imprisonment. Further, imprisonment, as described in the Webbs' book, he considered to be "a worse crime than any of those committed by its victims; for no single criminal can be as powerful for evil, or as unrestrained in its exercise, as an organized nation."

Shaw was notoriously polemical but he treated the Webbs' book with the gravity it deserved. Imprisonment is, of course, only one arm of punishment but with the abolition of both the death penalty and punishments little better than torture it is the most climactic in its impact on the offender and the society of which he is a member. Hence, we may ask if imprisonment is a force for good or if it produces predominately evil consequences?

More widely, what is the purpose, or what are the aims, of the institution of punishment in general and to what extent does it have a political dimension? In the main, three objects are usually proposed. First, deterrence, both of the criminal himself and of others tempted to commit crimes. Secondly, rehabilitation of the offender. Thirdly, retribution or vengeance. Many people accept the validity of one or two of these but rarely all three. Clearly, Shaw believed none of them to be acceptable or viable although his own solution of a better society and a new type of man appears somewhat remote.

In the meantime, in 1974, in *R. v. Sargeant,*[1] Lawton LJ, suggested that individual deterrence is rarely worth pursuing and the 1990 White Paper, *Crime, Justice and Protecting the Public,* accepted that prison does not reform. The Criminal Justice Act, 1991 which followed gives prominence to "just deserts" for the offender being primary in determining punishments. In other words, a form of retribution. In doing so, the Act, which has encroached on the hitherto acclaimed judicial independence in sentencing, has set aside the Gladstone Report's aims of deterrence and reform so far as imprisonment is concerned.

In any event, however, can these three objectives be seen as the whole story? Or are there other, less visible, motives for punishment? It cannot be denied that crime and punishment vary according to time and place as Bentham illustrated. They change with different levels of economic development, with changing cultural and social traditions and patterns of behaviour, with the needs of a given society and with the will of its governing class who make the law, define crime and determine punishments. They are also conceived differently for individuals according to their status in the political society as we have seen, for example, with the Game Laws and the Waltham Black Act.

History reveals that those who create punishments and

---

1.   60 Cr.App.R. 74.

those who execute them are all creatures of their own times. The punishment for rape has been severe or lenient in different ages. Some activities which were not crimes in the past but have been made so today include drug abuse, white-collar crimes, "drink driving" and some kinds of pollution of the environment. Punishments for gambling, debt and for sexual immorality such as adultery were severe in the Puritan Commonwealth but are relaxed today, if they exist at all.

Witches and Protestants are no longer burnt at the stake or, indeed, punished at all. The mere idea would seem ludicrous to the modern mind. Nevertheless, not only ancient lawgivers, but also such influential writers on penal law as Bentham and Stephen, have proceeded in the belief that punishments should be brought to bear on moral as well as legal guilt and this view has persisted until recent times and, indeed, still exists.

Another viewpoint is that as it is one of the foundations on which ordered society rests, any system of criminal law and punishment must depend upon subtle methods of coercion, and *in extremis* upon force, for its survival. Further questions therefore arise. Is there an ethic or philosophy of punishment? Does it somehow give guidance to people as to their conduct? Alternatively, is punishment merely a fluid, *ad hoc* means of social control of the dangerous and politically dissident elements in society?

Hugo Grotius defined punishment as, "the infliction of an ill for an ill done"[2] which tells us nothing about who is responsible for the punishing and why. It does, however, presuppose a victim who is in a subordinate position to the punisher. Clearly, in the Middle Ages, social control by the rulers of the day was to the fore and punishments crudely reflected that fact. Subsequently the philosophers of the Enlightenment concentrated on

---

2.   *De Jure Belli ac Pacis.* 1625.

humanism and society's duty to protect the rights of man, property and personal welfare against the brutality of the still dominant feudal penal laws and institutions. This was based on the secular social-contract theory which was expressed by Cesare Beccaria in the following words:

> Laws are the conditions, under which men, naturally independent, united themselves in society. Weary of living in a continual state of war, and of enjoying a liberty which became of little value, from the uncertainty of its duration, they sacrificed one part of it, to enjoy the rest in peace and security. The sum of all these portions of liberty of each individual constituted the sovereignty of a nation; and was deposited in the hands of the sovereign, as the lawful administrator. But it was not sufficient only to establish this deposit; it was also necessary to defend it from the usurpation of each individual, who would always endeavour not only to take away from the mass his own portion, but to encroach on that of others. Some motives, therefore, that strike the senses, were necessary to prevent the despotism of each individual from plunging society into its former chaos. Such motives are the punishments established against the transgressors of the laws.[3]

Some modern writers, such as H.E. Acton, support this emphasis on rights, calling in aid John Stuart Mill's opinion that punishment is justifiable only as a means of reforming the offender and securing the just rights of others. On this view, punishment by the state presupposes a system of publicly supported rights which some individuals may violate. Acton further makes the far-reaching claim that punishments are a valuable aid

---

3.   *Op. cit.* 5, 6.

to the moral education of the community.[4]

Similarly, A.C. Ewing has proposed an educative theory of punishment arguing that its pain shows the offender that he has acted wrongly. This, he says, will both help him to reform and act as a deterrent to him and others. The criminal will abstain from crime from moral motives. Indeed, the ideal punishment would be simply moral condemnation, but a penalty is also required to deter.[5]

In sharp contrast Michel Foucault has claimed that, whilst public executions underlined the power of the State, the convict prisons of the nineteenth century were designed to create fear in order to break the spirits (instead of the bodies) of the working class, and to reduce its law-breakers to inadequates who were socially harmless.[6] Presumably, however, they would have had to achieve this by the open show of power.

Edward Thompson and Douglas Hay also see eighteenth century pre-industrial penal law as an important element in class rule, with its arbitrary power restrained only by the need for legitimacy to ensure its durability by consent.[7] This, they argue, gives law its own characteristics and in the eighteenth century it existed in its own rights as ideology which both served and legitimized class power. Fearsome punishments for offences, both serious and trivial, together with the ritual display of the majesty of the law at Assize towns, but with a degree of equality before the law, were integral parts of this process.

Michael Ignatieff in a recent essay in *Social Control and the State*[8] admits to three misconceptions as to punishment and power to be found in his book *A Just*

---

4.   *The Philosophy of Punishment.* ed. 16. 65. 1969.
5.   *Morality of Punishment.* 1929.
6.   *Discipline and Punishment. The Birth of the Prison.* 1979.
7.   Thompson. *Op. cit.* ch.10, and Hay: *Albion's Fatal Tree*, ch.1.
8.   Ed. Stanley Cohen. 1983.

Measure of Pain.[9] These were that the state has a
monopoly over punitive regulation of behaviour; that its
authority and power bind the social order; and that all
social relations can be described in language of
subordination. Such a view was too simplistic.

However, despite his re-appraisal, that is precisely the
situation as it appeared to Sir James Fitzjames Stephen.
For Stephen, force had been an essential arm of the state
throughout history and those who owned property and
controlled the State have always enacted laws to
determine what acts and omissions should be crimes.
Coercion, he said, was a virtue which had built up all the
great churches and nations. And it had not disappeared
with the growth of civilization. Abraham Lincoln, for
example, commanded a force which would have crushed
Charlemagne and his paladins like so many eggshells.
What is more, parliamentary government is only a mild
and disguised form of compulsion.[10]

But this last point touches on a crucial element. As we
have seen throughout this book the Sovereign, the Church
and the State have at various times played a vital role
in naming what should be crimes and punishments. But
does the modern state comprise only like-minded persons
adopting a coherent strategy to maintain their rule? Or
are there conflicts and tensions in determining a penal
policy and should we not see its primary aim as resolving
social frictions? Such questions form the essence of a
continuing debate and need to be addressed.

The Perspective of History

Stephen saw the history of punishments as the most

---

9.   *Op. cit.*
10.   *Liberty, Equality, Fraternity.* 19. 184. 30. 2nd edn. 1873.

curious part of the history of the criminal law.[11] Presumably because of its tangled web of cruelty and anomaly. To commence with early Anglo-Saxon times, we see that the customs of private vengeance were the product of a harsh and unstable society. Hence, as the wealth and power of the kings and the Church expanded, they desired a less violent and more stable and cohesive society which would be easier to control. This would also ensure for them a continuing expansion of their respective landholdings and incomes.

However, medieval Christianity came to put greater emphasis on the responsibility of the individual wrongdoer. As well as being a criminal he was seen to sin against the law of God. Nevertheless he also had a soul to be saved. Not that this prevented the Church from exercising great cruelty and torture, arguing that it was necessary to avoid the greater and permanent suffering in hell.

Retribution remained an essential ingredient of punishment but it was also required to deter. These twin aims, together with the need to avoid popular discontent and even uprisings, gave rise to the desirability of a system of laws which would lay down rules of conduct to which the population could assent. Religion and the quasi-democratic communal courts were also required to play their part in ensuring legitimacy and such support. Nonetheless, the State was always prepared to use force and violence to enforce the laws in order to maintain, guide and regulate behaviour.

This latter use of punishments persisted throughout the Middle Ages with considerable coercion to ensure its success, but always with an eye to securing public consent. Apart from the very important financial considerations which influenced the monarchs of this

---

11.   *Op. cit.* i. 457.

period they rarely forgot that they needed at least the consent, and preferably the support, of powerful people - the barons, landowners and higher clergy - to keep the common people in their place.

To this end they were prepared to encourage the growth of a common law, a legal system and a profession. They also accepted trial by jury which had an important stabilizing function in all parts of the land and in which the wealthy participated as jurors. The system of private vengeance had been replaced by one based on individual responsibility for wrongdoing.

To some extent the Tudors and Stuarts broke the pattern by ending baronial feuds, and establishing a monopoly of "corrective violence" which was one factor giving rise to the Commonwealth. However, after the traumas of the Civil War, Puritan rule and the military dictatorship of the Major-Generals the Crown was again permitted a large measure of power. Hence Sir Robert Filmer was to be found in 1680 re-asserting the Divine Right of Kings and explaining that the laws of England were simply the expression of the king's will since he could amend them or abrogate them at his discretion.[12]

Nevertheless, following the Glorious Revolution, the propertied classes enlarged their share in power in order to protect their extensive estates and privileges. Juries were no more democratically selected than before but they became more independent. So too did the Judges who henceforth were removable only upon an address of both Houses of Parliament. However, paradoxically, and precisely in order to secure their interests from rebellion by the common people, a great many men of property were prepared to accept the authority of the king provided he was contained by their Constitution. This, they

---

12.   *Patriarcha and other Political Works of Sir Robert Filmer.* ed. P. Laslett. 62. 1949.

thought, would secure their legitimacy and avoid the use of force for social control.

Unfortunately, oligarchy reared its head and, as a prelude to the Waltham Black Act and the "Bloody Code" of the eighteenth century, statutes added shoplifting and stealing by lodgers to the list of crimes punishable by death. Housebreaking too was made capital because, as Blackstone put it, of "improvements in trade and opulence."[13] And the extent of the severity of punishment was greatly increased by the creation of new felonies without benefit of clergy.

Yet the earlier methods of class control and discipline were beginning to prove less effective, with a growth of sympathy for the poor and the "pious perjury" of juries. So they were strengthened with the example of terror. Walpole, and his nouveau-riche friends used the penalty of death as a political weapon and, like President Richard Nixon in our time, promoted a "law and order" policy which was based on unlawful acts and corruption.

One reason for this was that the agriculture of the landed gentry had become capital-based and their power uncontrolled. As one writer has put it:

> Their rents swelled with the demand for farm-produce, the expansion of cities (whose soil they owned) and of mines, forges and railways (which were situated on their estates) ... Their social predominance remained untouched, their political power in the countryside complete, and even in the nation not seriously troubled ...[14]

Little wonder Walter Bagehot complained that Parliament had exhibited "an undue bias towards the

---

13.   *Op. cit.* iv. 240.
14.   E.J. Hobsbawm. *Industry and Empire.* 62. 1969.

sentiments and views of the landed interest," adding that "the series of Cabinet Ministers presents a nearly unbroken rank of persons who either are themselves large landowners, or are connected closely by birth or inter-marriage with large landowners."[15]

This eighteenth century ruling class was small in number and was used to relying upon its own retainers to protect its spacious local lands and wealth. But to safeguard its national power from the consequences of instability and disorder it greatly extended the operation of the death penalty for offences against property, tempered, as we have seen, by the use of discretion and pardons in implementing it.

As Douglas Hay has written, "the law made enough examples to inculcate fear, but not so many as to harden or repel a populace that had to assent, in some measure at least, to the rule of property."[16] And that assent is largely what was achieved, with the ordinary citizens identifying with the rule of law as providing some means of justice. The rule of law was far removed from being seen as merely an expression of naked, arbitrary power. Particularly when compared with the odious system the common people saw across the Channel where breaking on the wheel, burning, and tearing the flesh with red-hot pincers were commonplace.

Leniency in Punishment

What then caused the period of the "Bloody Code" to come to an end in the nineteenth century? In the first place the Industrial Revolution brought prosperity for many and the use of force and terror to inculcate fear were no longer

---

15.   *Essays on Parliamentary Reform.* 12, 209. 1883.
16.   *Albion's Fatal Tree. Op. cit.* 57.

seen by the ruling class as such pressing necessities. Another consequence of that revolution had been the emergence of a powerful and militant middle class and a movement for parliamentary and penal reform.

On behalf of this new style middle class, James Mill made a ferocious attack on government by aristocracy in his *Essay on Government,* written for the *Encyclopedia Britannica* in 1818 but reprinted for a wider audience in 1820. At the same time the Essay was a call to the middle class to see itself as the leader of society and the guardian of the people against tyranny. He wrote of the middling class as he called it:

> It contains beyond all comparison, the greatest proportion of the intelligence, industry, and wealth of the state. In it are the heads that invent, and the hands that execute; the enterprise that projects, and the capital by which these projects are carried into operation ... The people of the class below are the instruments with which they work; and those of the class above, though they may be called their governors, and may really sometimes seem to rule them, are much more often, more truly, and more completely under their control. In this country at least, it is this class which gives to the nation its character.

This appeal to the middle class to take over the political hegemony of society from the aristocracy was precisely what many of its members wanted to hear. And as part of the powerful and political change this involved they wanted less severity and more certainty in the criminal law in order to protect their type of wealth in the fields of commerce and business.

At the same time we have seen the humanitarian influences of reformers such as Beccaria and Bentham which had a profound effect on the press and the middle-class element of public opinion. The Enlightenment, a new sensitivity to violence in punishment and the Social Contract theory, also a reflection of the emergence of modern capitalist society, likewise encouraged more lenient punishments.

In the early twentieth century, Emile Durkheim has advanced the theory that punishments become more lenient as society moves from primitive to advanced status.[17] Foucault has more or less taken a similar position as far as industrialized societies are concerned. The death penalty and severity for all have been replaced by individualized means of control of criminals. According to Durkheim, crime is normal because a society exempt from it is utterly impossible. Furthermore, crime has become necessary for the normal evolution of morality and law since it forces changes that prevent them becoming rigid and useless.[18] Hence, only law-breakers who threaten the established rule need be neutralized.

Also, says Durkheim elevating the proposition to a "Law," deprivation of liberty and of liberty alone, varying in time according to the seriousness of the crime, tends to become more and more the normal means of social control. In other words prisons become warehouses to keep deviants out of society. The vengeance of the sovereign, adds Foucault, has shifted to the defence of society.[19]

The impact of the industrial revolution had led to the differences revealed in the ruling class in the nineteenth century over the relative claims made for ordinary imprisonment on the one hand and the penitentiary on the other. The belief that solitary confinement would lead

---

17.   *Two Laws of Penal Evolution.* 1973 edn.
18.   Durkheim. *Rules of Sociological Method.* 70. 1950.
19.   *Op. cit.* 90.

to reformation did not appeal to everyone. But industrial society needed a more efficient control of the individuals it confined to prisons than the lax - and thereby inhuman - methods of the past. Furthermore, in addition to the desire for leniency the growth of large towns and cities had made terror and the former methods of control ineffective.

The emergence of the new police forces from 1829 onwards meant penalties could be both more appropriate to the crime and more uniformly enforced instead of simply physically cruel and arbitrary. Henceforth the poor law and the criminal law were to deal with each offender as an individual, although with scant sympathy for him. Rehabilitation of the offender was the new message, to replace Paley-like deterrence by the discretionary infliction of death on something like one in 10 of those convicted of capital felonies.

Nevertheless, the objective of social control remained prominent with a constant interplay between regulating behaviour and the protection of a vastly increased community. A more complex industrial society and the emergence of democracy demanded a more bureaucratic national structure of control and more sophisticated punishments. At all times these were determined by political motives. Nonetheless, there was always conflict as to the precise form of punishments to be invoked, both within the governing class itself and between it and the middle and working classes. As a consequence of deep-rooted pressures from all sides, as well as a continuing and complex requirement of democratic legitimacy, there could be no simplistic or unified ruling class conspiracy.

In the event, nineteenth century prisons isolated the criminal class from the general working class. The apologia for this was revealed when Sir Archibald Alison claimed that nine-tenths of all crime was committed by members of the lowest class in society; 150,000 persons,

he wrote, were annually involved in committing crimes.
That is 150,000 from the three million who comprised the
"lowest and most squalid classes." For the remainder
there were only 30,000 criminals from the 24 million who
lived in comparative comfort.[20]

What was needed was discipline through law, effective
policing to stem the rising tide of crime and disorder and
protect urban middle-class property, and the industry-
induced Protestant work ethic. The new penitentiary-type
prisons were meant to provide just such a disciplined
environment. The patent failure of the inhuman
penitentiary, however, combined with a determined effort
to reconcile the incompatible aims of deterrence,
retribution and reform, inevitably resulted in a belated
search for yet another fresh philosophy of punishment in
the late nineteenth century.

Ethical Issues

Here we can return to ethics and the philosophy of
punishment. If we go back to Aristotle we find the view
that just retribution involves a proportional reprisal. In
other words a fair correlation between offence and
punishment, ie, justice. Punishment, to Aristotle, was
effected by means of pleasures and pains and was to be
a kind of remedial treatment to produce moral goodness.
It was to have an educational function.[21]

Sir Walter Moberly, a writer on the ethics of
punishment, firmly believes that the moral quality of
punishment lies in its intrinsic justice rather than in its
possible effect in causing or averting pain.[22] Sir James

---

20.   *Blackwood's Edinburgh Magazine. Op. cit.*
21.   *Ethics.* Penguin Classics. 95. 183. 1976 edn.
22.   *The Ethics of Punishment.* 1968.

Fitzjames Stephen, on the other hand, firmly believed in the morality of retribution and even judicial vengeance. He wrote: "The criminal law proceeds upon the principle that it is morally right to hate criminals, and it confirms and justifies that sentiment by inflicting upon criminals punishments which express it."[23]

He continued by asserting that the primary object of legal punishments was "the direct prevention of crime, either by fear, or by disabling or even destroying the offender ... Death, flogging and the like emphatically justify and gratify the public desire for vengeance upon such offenders as justify exemplary punishments."[24]

Edward Livingston was an outstanding American penal reformer and architect of the Criminal Code of Louisiana which had a profound influence on later such codes in the United States. In 1831, echoing Thucydides, he wrote of punishments:

> All the variety of pains that the body of man could suffer, infamy and death, have figured as sanctions in the codes of all nations; but although these have been in a train of experiment for thousands of years, under every form that government, manners and religion could give, they have never produced the expected effect.[25]

Most punishments, Livingston explained, produced in the victim a spirit of hatred, revenge and a desire to retaliate on society. He was opposed to retribution and as he considered severity had no more general deterrent effect than lesser punishments he took a position

---

23.   *Op. cit.* ii. 81.
24.   *Ibid.* 83.
25.   *Remarks on the Expediency of Abolishing the Punishment of Death.* Philadelphia.

diametrically opposed to that of Stephen.

Bentham, whom Livingston greatly admired, thought, as we have seen in relation to imprisonment, that the pain of punishment should be utilitarian in that it should both reform the prisoner and act as a deterrent to him and others. The welfare of the prisoner was to be promoted but his fate must also be a warning to others. Thus all punishments had to be dreaded or they could not effect their purpose.[26] They were a form of political control meant to prevent more evil than they produced. Retribution was not acceptable.

John Locke considered that history proved that government could only be viable if created by consent. Men give up their natural state in return for a government that will establish laws for the public good, appoint impartial Judges and preserve law and order in the community.[27] The ensuing political power gives the right to create the penalty of death, and hence all lesser ones. For Romilly, later, a claim to legitimacy was a most formidable element in power, but he would not have denied that it was affected by changing complex social arrangements.

Some modern criminologists argue that the approach of Locke and Beccaria, far from being humanist, is contrary to humanism. It accepts the power but wants merely to dilute its effects. It also accepts the existing distribution of property on which power to rule is based whereas what is required is social ownership and better human relationships. They see capitalism as a contradictory society in which social conditioning is the cause of criminality and deviance is normal in asserting human diversity.[28] There may be something worthwhile

---

26. *Works* i. 412.
27. *Two Treatises.* ii. 95-131.
28. *The New Criminology. For a Social Theory of Deviance.* 1973.

in studying the response of society to criminal behaviour but, as with George Bernard Shaw, their alleged solution of a new socialistic society does not seem to be imminent.

Some modern punishments such as compensation orders, where the offender pays towards the loss, damage or personal injury suffered by the victim, and community service orders may rightly be seen as having an educational function. Compensation may induce in the offender an understanding of the personality and rights of others. Similarly, unpaid community services is not merely a deprivation of freedom for a given number of hours, it also involves reparation to the community which invokes a moral principle. It seems clear, however, that educative and moral aims are not the primary purpose of punishment in the last resort.

Social Control?

Legal punishment undoubtedly flows from the power of the state. That power is underpinned by the threat of coercion which exists even though it may be obscured by the more visible fabric of consent. The state alone wields the apparatus of social control - the police, the criminal and penal law, the media, and ultimately the armed forces. Nevertheless, all of these are affected by the responses of people within them and outside, which is why dictatorships which appear to be all-powerful and permanent can be overthrown.

As we have suggested, conflicts over social control exist not least within the governing class and its supporters. This does not mean, however, that social control is not the primary objective of punishments.

A modern analogy might be with the policy of appeasement of Neville Chamberlain's government in the 1930s leading up to World War II. Differences in the government are known to have existed, and indeed Foreign Secretary Anthony Eden resigned over them. But still the policy of appeasement obtained until the war broke out. The government managed to contain dissent in its ranks and would not permit within itself alternative approaches undermining that principal aim.

Yet is the analogy apposite? In terms of the criminal law and punishments the State has to take into account the courts, lay magistrates and juries, rules of evidence and proof, as well as the legal ideology of the rights of "free-born Englishmen." But aberrations exist. As recently as 1961 startling claims were made by Lord Parker, then Lord Chief Justice, which were reminiscent of pronouncements made by Tudor and Stuart Judges, with the honourable exceptions of Coke and Hale. Lord Parker, in a prominent trial, asserted that "the citizen's highest duty is to the State." He went further, on another occasion, in declaring that the judiciary is the handmaiden of the executive.

More recently, and on the other side of the same coin, *The Times* of May 1, 1993, revealed that the release of confidential documents by Mr Justice Smedley in the Matrix Churchill trial at the Old Bailey had led some Ministers to question the powers of the judiciary where the "national interest" is at stake. Such views from members of the Cabinet, *The Times* added, could lead to attempts to change the balance of power between the executive and the judiciary which, it suggested, would lead to uproar.

These attitudes breathe a spirit entirely foreign to our modern democratic traditions. In a highly industrialized democracy, capitalist rule depends even more than in societies of the past on the consent of the ruled. The people now have more power than ever before in consequence of the education they have had to be given if the country is to survive in an advanced technological age. To this must be added the pressures they can assert with the franchise, trade unions and numerous pressure groups. The media, the Church and the school system help to sustain the established rules of the existing social order in principle, and in a general manner, but not in detail and only if they themselves enjoy popular support which also has to be actively sought.

It would appear, therefore, that punishment remains ultimately an instrument of control by the governing class and has done so throughout history. But it also plays an important, and more visible, role in safeguarding security and order for the community. The acceptance by the State of the institutionalization of crime in society means that this latter function is to some extent undermined so far as some members of the public are concerned, in particular victims and those who perceive themselves to be potential victims of criminal activity. This is, however, marginal in the sense that no general breakdown of the rule of law is likely.

What is clear is that in both the above-mentioned aspects punishment is fulfilling a political function that is an integral strand in the wide, complex tapestry of modern society.

BIBLIOGRAPHY

A.   *Manuscript Sources*

(1)   *British Museum. Additional MSS.*
Bentham Papers. 33109:33533.
Peel Correspondence with Lord Lyndhurst. 40442.

(2)   *Public Record Office*
HO 13/68. Petitions for Pardons.
HO 144/1002/134165. Preventive Detention.
HO Cmd. 5684. Corporal Punishment.

B.   *Parliamentary Papers*

Report of Select Committee on Criminal Law. PP. (1828)
VI. 12.
The 1833 Criminal Law Commissioners' Second Report.
PP. (1836) XXXVI, 138.
Third Report. (1837) PP. XXXI. 1.
Lord John Russell Correspondence with the Criminal Law
Commissioners. PP (1837) XXI. 31.
Two Reports from the House of Lords Select Committee
on Juvenile Offenders and Transportation. (1847). PP.
VIII.
Report to the Law Commission on Codification of the
Criminal Law. (1985). Law Com. 143.
Hansard: 1812-1870.

C.   *Other Reports and Collections*

Report on Inquiry into the Hulks at Woolwich. (1847).
    XLVIII.
Criminal Code of Louisiana. (1873 edn).
Report of the Departmental Committee on Prisons.
    (1895). C. 2nd ser. 7703.

D.   *Printed Sources*

(1)   *Newspapers*
            The Times

(2)   *Journals*
            American Journal of Legal History, ii. 1967.
            Blackwood's Edinburgh Magazine, July 1844.
            Edinburgh Review, 1813.
            Justice of the Peace, 1992.
            Law Magazine, 1823-41.
            Law Quarterly Review, 1890.
            London and Westminster Review, 1838.
            Northern Ireland Legal Quarterly, 1973.
            The Saturday Review, 1862.
            The Tatler, 1709.

(3)   *Contemporary Books, Pamphlets and Articles*

Alison, A. "Causes of the Increase of Crime." *Blackwood's
    Edinburgh Magazine*. LVI. (July 1844).
Amos, Andrew. *The Ruins of Time exemplified in Sir
    Matthew Hale's Pleas of the Crown*. (1856).
Andrews, H.B. *Criminal Law: Being a Commentary on
    Bentham on Death Punishment*. (1833).
Aristotle. *Ethics*. Penguin Classics (1976 edn.).

Bagehot, Walter. *Essays on Parliamentary Reform.* (1883).

Beccaria, Cesare. *Dei Delitti e delle Pene.* (1769).

Bentham, Jeremy. *Works* 11 vols. (1843).
  Essay on the Influence of Time and Place. Works. i. 169.
  Rationale of Punishment. (1830).
  Memoirs and Correspondence. Works. x. 1-606. xi. 1-170.
  Panopticon, or, The Inspection House. Works. iv. 37.

Birks, T.R. *Modern Utilitarianism.* (1874).

Blackstone, William (Sir). *The Commentaries on the Laws of England.* vol.4 (1876).

Bowring, John. *Memoirs of Jeremy Bentham.* (1843).

Bracton. *De Legibus.* (1250).

Brougham, Henry (Lord). *Speeches.* (1838).

Coke, Edward (Sir). *Third Institute.* (1644).
  Second Institute. (1644).
  Reports. (1602).

Eden, William. *Principles of Penal Law.* (1771).

Fielding, Henry. *A Proposal for Making an Effectual Provision for the Poor etc.* (1753).

Fortescue. *De Laudibus.* (1470).

Goldsmith, Oliver. *The Vicar of Wakefield.* (1852).

Grotius, Hugo. *De Jure Belli ac Pacis.* (1625).

Hale, Matthew (Sir). *The History of the Pleas of the Crown.* 2 vols. (1736).

Howard, John. *The State of the Prisons etc.* (1780).

Jardine, David. *A Reading on the Use of Torture in the Criminal Law of England prior to the Commonwealth.* (1836).

Laud (Monk). *Anglo-Saxon Chronicle*. (1953 edn.).

Livingston, Edward. *Remarks on the Expediency of Abolishing the Punishment of Death*. (1831).

Locke, John. *An Essay Concerning the True, Original, Extent and End of Civil Government*. (1689).

Lonsdale, B.M. *Statute Criminal Law*. (1839).

Madan, Martin. *Thoughts on Executive Justice*. (1785).

Maine, Henry. *Early History of Institutions*. (1875).

Mill, James. *Essay on Government*. (1818).

Mill, John Stuart. "Bentham" *London and Westminster Review*. (1838).

Montague, J. Basil. *Thoughts on the Punishment of Death for Forgery*. (1831).

North, Roger. *Life of the Late Lord Keeper Guilford*. (1742).

Paley, William. *Principles of Moral and Political Philosophy*. (1786).

Pike, L.O. *A History of Crime in England*. (1876).

Pollock and Maitland. *The History of English Law*. 2 vols. (1895).

Romilly, Samuel (Sir). *Observations on a Late Publication*. (1786).
   Speeches. (1820).
   Memoirs. (1840).

Russell, W.O. (Sir). *On Crimes*. (1865).

Rutt, J.T. ed. *The Diary of Thomas Burton Esq*. (1889).

Smollett, G.T. *The History of England*. (1794).

State Tryals. (1719) edn.).

State Trials. (1735 edn.)

Stephen, James Fitzjames (Sir). *Liberty, Equality, Fraternity.* (1873).
"The Criminal Code." *The Nineteenth Century.* (1880).
History of the Criminal Law of England. 3 vols. (1883).
"Essays by a Barrister." *The Saturday Review.* (1862).

Wrightson, Thomas. *On the Punishment of Death.* (1837).

(4)   *Modern Books, Pamphlets and Articles*

Abbott, W.C. ed. *The Writings and Speeches of Oliver Cromwell.* (1937-47).
Acton, H.B. *The Philosophy of Punishment.* (1969).
Ashworth, Andrew. *Sentencing and Criminal Justice.* (1993).
Andrews, Wm. *Bygone Punishments.* (1931).
Attenborough, F. *Laws of the Earliest English Kings.* (1922).

Babington, A. *The Rule of Law in Britain.* (1978).
The Power to Silence. A History of Punishment in Britain. (1968).
Bailey, V. ed. *Policing and Punishments in Nineteenth Century Britain.* (1981).
Bellamy, J.G. *The Law of Treason in the Later Middle Ages.* (1970).

Cohen, S. ed. *Social Control and the State.* (1983).
Cornish, W.R. "Criminal Justice and Punishment." In *Crime and Law in Nineteenth Century Britain.* (1978).
Cross, Rupert. *Punishment, Prison and the Public.* (1971).

Durkheim, E. *Two Laws of Penal Evolution.* (1973 edn.).
Rules of Sociological Method. (1950).

Ewing, A.C. *Morality of Punishment.* (1929).

Foucault, Michel. *Discipline and Punishment. The Birth of the Prison.* (1979).

Fox, Lionel W. *The English Prison and Borstal Systems.* (1952).

Gash, Norman. *Mr Secretary Peel.* (1961).

Hart, H.L.A. "Bentham and Demystification of the Law." 36 *M.L.R.* (1973).

Hay, Douglas. "Property, Authority and the Criminal Law." In *Albion's Fatal Tree.* (1975).

Hobsbawm, E.J. *Industry and Empire.* (1969).

Holdsworth, William (Sir). *A History of English Law.* 16 vols. (1903-66).

"Sir Matthew Hale." 39 *LQR.* (1923).

Hostettler, John. *The Politics of Criminal Law: Reform in the Nineteenth Century.* (1992).

Thomas Wakley. An Improbable Radical. (1993).

Ignatieff, Michael. *A Just Measure of Pain.* (1989).

Ives, G. *A History of Penal Methods.* (1914).

Keeton, G.W. *Ld. Chancellor Jeffreys and the Stuart Cause.* (1965).

Laslett, P. ed. *Patriarcha and other Political Works of Sir Robert Filmer.* (1949).

Milsom, S.F.C. *Historical Foundations of the Common Law.* (1969).

Moberly, Walter (Sir). *The Ethics of Punishment.* (1968).

Ogg, David. *England in the Reign of Charles II.* (1967).

Parry, L.A. *History of Torture in England.* (1933).
Peters, E. *Torture.* (1985).
Pettifer, E. *Punishments of Former Days.* (1992).
Playfair, Giles. *The Primitive Obsession.* (1971).

Robertson, A.J. *The Laws of the Kings of England from Edmund to Henry I.* (1925).
Radzinowicz, Leon (Sir). *A History of English Criminal Law.* 5 vols. (1948-86).
"Sir James Fitzjames Stephen 1829-1894." *Selden Society.* (1959).

Saleilles, R. *Individualization of Punishment.* (1911).
Shaw, A.G.L. *Convicts and Colonies.* (1966).
Sheehan, W.J. "Finding Solace in Eighteenth Century Newgate." In: *Crime in England 1550-1800.* ed. J.S. Cockburn. (1977).
Skyrme, T. (Sir). *The History of the Justices of the Peace.* 3 vols. (1991).
Smith, Harry. "From Deodand to Dependency." 11 *American Journal of Legal History.* (1967).
Speck, W.A. *Stability and Strife. England 1714-1760.* (1977).
Spierenburg, P. *The Spectacle of Suffering.* (1984).
Stenton, F.M. *Anglo-Saxon England.* (1985).

Taylor, Walker & Young. *The New Criminology. For a Social Theory of Deviance.* (1973).
Thompson, E.P. *Whigs and Hunters. The Origin of the Black Act.* (1975).
Twining, W.L. "Bentham on Torture." 24 *Northern Ireland Legal Quarterly.* (1973).

Veall, D. *The Popular Movement for Law Reform 1640-1660.* (1970).

Walker, Nigel. *Crime and Insanity in England.* (1968).
Webb, S. & B. *English Prisons under Local Government.* (1922).

INDEX

CASES CITED